Rail-Trail
Handbook

MN

Rail-Trail Handbook

The Most Complete
Guide to Rail-Trails
For Hiking, Biking,
In-Line Skating *and more*

UPPER MIDWEST REGION
Northern Iowa
Minnesota
Western Wisconsin

DISCARDED

By Bruce B. Blair

NODIN PRESS
MINNEAPOLIS

ISBN 0-931714-71-0

Nodin Press, a division of Micawber's, Inc.
525 North Third Street
Minneapolis, MN 55401

Cover photo by: Stephanie Torbert

Maps by: Bruce B. Blair, and
            Stanton Publication Services, Inc., St. Paul, MN

Dedication

This book is dedicated to those who make rail-trails
possible: individuals who inspire; communities who
organize and cooperate; governments that support;
and the trail user, because using them makes
them work.

Acknowledgments

The author visited every trail that has a detailed description in this guide and was always received cordially by people interested in rail-trails. He thanks them all. A special thanks to the Minnesota Department of Natural Resources, the Wisconsin Department of Natural Resources, the northern Iowa County Conservation Boards and the Rails-to-Trails Conservancy of Washington, D.C.

Preface

There is something about rail-trails that makes sense.
Maybe it has to do with the inherent appropriateness
of exchanging something that can no longer be— a
railroad line—into America's new favorite outdoor
place—a rail-trail.

These kinds of trails are not new. The Harry Cook
Nature Trail at Osage, Iowa, was used as a walking
path to the river as early as 1900. The Elroy-Sparta
State Park Trail in Wisconsin got going in the late
1960's, a full decade ahead of nearly everywhere else.

What is new is the growth, popularity, and success
of rail-trails, especially in the Midwest, because these
trails satisfy our recreational needs for a quality experience close to home. We have less time to recreate
than before and want to strengthen our affinity with
family and landscape, to experience a sense of well-
being that we have been somewhere and done something that matters. The 53 described and 56 additional
trails within these pages do that.

This *Rail-Trail Handbook* is designed to get you to the
trail and headed in the direction that's right for you.

Contents

TRAILS

4: **Rail-Trails of Western Wisconsin**

1:
New Trails on Old Rails

It's not hard to imagine that the first trails of the upper Midwest might have been created by Native Americans as they migrated in response to seasonal needs and a landscape changed by the Ice Ages. Eventually came European explorers following the rivers, ridges, and ecological boundaries. Soon pioneers flooded in, developing more trails, then roads. By the Civil War railroads were established as far west as Illinois, eventually creating a network all over the upper Midwest. This network became the world's largest by 1916 with over 300,000 miles in operation. In the Midwest virtually every town of any size had a railroad or risked economic stagnation, as the railroad carried the timber, the crops, the ore, the supplies, and the people building a nation.

There were problems, however. Some lines were built for competition purposes, not for any anticipated profit from business on the line. Other routes served places that had declined because of exhaustion of timber, ore or soil. The automobile was capturing the country's transportation fantasy. The rail system begin to contract, and abandonments became common in the 1930's. Passenger service declined after World War II and by the late 1960's was almost extinct except in major cities and a few routes between. Freight moved more by truck than by train. The contraction continues, and today less than one-half of the peak mileage remains. The abandonment process proceeds at a rate of over 2,000 miles a year, with much of the loss in the Midwest, where perhaps the rail system was most over-built.

These losses have presented an opportunity for a new kind of public place called rail-trails. Rail-trails involve the conversion of a disused and legally abandoned railroad right-of-way into a linear place for people to recreate. Rail-trails include benefits such as the preservation of habitat and historic sites, safeguarding imperiled plant and animal species, and connecting neighborhoods. As our country's transportation needs grow and mature, it is clear that rail-trails are part of the solution.

In the Midwest the rails-to-trails movement traces its origin to a letter written to the editor of the *Chicago Tribune* in 1963 by the late naturalist May Theilgaard Watts. She proposed a trail from the western Chicago suburbs on abandoned right-of-way. Her letter inspired the creation of the Illinois Prairie Path, now 55 miles long. Other rail-trails followed, at first slowly, often with controversy. Now a new trail opens up every week somewhere in the country. At last count, according to the Rails-to-Trails Conservancy of Washington, D.C., there were 732 rail-trails, totaling 7,606 miles dispersed among 48 states. *Rail-Trail Handbook* describes 53 trails occupying 1,019 miles of rail bed and mentions 56 more, totaling 944 miles for a combined length of 1,963 miles.

The rail-trails described in this guide all have three things in common: they occupy a former railroad right-of-way, are publicly owned, and are available for some public recreational trail use. Levels of development and uses vary greatly. Three are set aside as prairie preserves where even picnicking is prohibited. Others have asphalt surfaces or allow a mix of motorized and non-motorized uses. Some rail-trails are inadvertent. A land acquisition within a state-park boundary may contain a rail bed-perfect for trail development in the park.

Management of rail-trails is diversifying. It used to be in Minnesota and Wisconsin that nearly every trail was established and managed by the state's Department of Natural Resources. This is no longer true, as public interest in rail-trails has surpassed the state's ability to provide. Citizens form associations to promote and establish a trail along with some sort of management structure, often at the county level. In Iowa, conservation and recreation have always been primarily the responsibility of local county conservation boards. This is true with rail-trails as well.

This diversity in ownership and management, while healthy, has made comparisons between trails more difficult. For example, a crushed-rock surface at one trail may be suitable for touring bicycles but not at another because of varying development or maintenance standards. Some trails allow pets; others do not. *Rail-Trail Handbook* provides the information needed to make comparisons.

Enjoying rail-trails and using recreational equipment is not without risks. The magnitude of the risks varies widely depending on such things as the condition of yourself, your equipment, and the trail; weather; the skill and behavior of other users; and

more. Plan ahead and don't hesitate to turn back.
Write or call for current information. Stay within your
abilities. Use all the protective gear appropriate for
your activity, such as helmets and wrist guards. Rail-
trails are not static. In river valleys they can be open
one day and flooded the next. Many trails are in the
process of being improved. This may mean the pres-
ence of construction equipment and even temporary
trail closure. Unfortunately, acts of vandalism can create unexpected hazards. A list of the unexpected
would be long and incomplete. You must take
personal responsibility for your safety!

Rail-Trails of the Upper Midwest

Bemidji

Duluth

Ashland

MINNESOTA

WIS CONSIN

(94)

(35)

(13)

**Eau
Claire**

Minneapolis

**St.
Paul**

(94)

**Wisconsin
Rapids**

Rochester

Mankato

(90)

(90)

Madison

Milwauk

(35)

Mon roe

Waterloo

Dubuque

(20)

IO WA

**Cedar
Rapids**

N

**Des
Moines**

| 0 | 50 | 100 |

Miles

/// Area covered by Rail-Trail Handbook

Text Explanation

The trail descriptions contain the following information:

Trail Name: Official name of the trail or segment of a longer trail.

Administered by: Entity responsible for management.

Primary: Refers to the treadway primarily occupying the area where the rails were.

Secondary: Refers to a treadway somewhere else in the corridor.

Symbols: The uses allowed on a treadway are identified by symbols. See map legend for more detail. The wheelchair symbol is used for asphalt, asphalt emulsion, and crushed-rock surfaces only when maintenance standards are high so that enjoyable use in a wheelchair is possible.

A treadway's surface is identified as one of the following:

Asphalt: usually 8–10 feet wide. Often suitable for all uses except horses.

Asphalt emulsion: road-type seal coating oil mixed with small diameter rock and applied to a crushed rock base. Generally suitable for touring bicycles but not in-line skates.

Crushed rock: when well maintained makes a satisfactory surface for most uses except in-line skating.

Limestone screenings: very fine crushed rock.

Natural surface: usually grass or dirt.

Original ballast: what the railroad used under the tracks and ties as a base. Often large diameter rock or cinders occasionally partially covered with grass or dirt.

FYI: For your information. Here you find any special or nontypical information useful in planning a trip.

Length: Total trail length in miles.

Fees: Fees that are required are listed here. This kind of information occasionally changes and the users should double-check at a major trail access.

Recommendation: Can't do the whole trail? Then look here for recommendations on where to start and what not to miss.

FMI: For more information. First is listed the address and phone number of the trail administrators, then the local chamber of commerce or other source of area information.

General Trail Character: An overview of the trail and the railroad history.

Trail Segment Descriptions/Access Details: Most often the trail is described from west to east and south to north beginning with access directions and facilities available. The following symbols are used to indicate which facilities are available:

⛟ Parking ⑤ Water

⋔ Picnic 🚽 Toilets

Note: Some facilities are seasonal.

Something Unique: At some trails there is an experience or place you must encounter for the best visit. Find it listed here.

More Trail: Many rail-trails connect to other kinds of trail / park opportunities, and new trails are coming on line constantly. If something like this is happening, you'll read about it here.

Map Legend

These symbols represent the described uses:

👥 hiking, walking, jogging, trail running allowed

🚲 bicycling allowed

🚵 mountain bicycles recommended

⛷ cross-country skiing allowed

🛼 in-line skating allowed

♿ wheelchair (and similar devices) reasonably possible

🛷 snowmobiles allowed

🚜 all terrain vehicles allowed

🐎 Horseback riding allowed

Other Map Symbols

Rail-Trail

━━━ Rail-Trail

⬯ Interstate Highway

⬡ U.S. Highway

◯ State Highway

▢ County Road

----- City-Limit Boundary

〰 Water (river, lake, etc.)

[I 1] Trail Identification Number

🚗 Parking

⊼ Picnic

🚻 Toilets

🚰 Drinking Water

2:
Rail-Trails of Northern Iowa

Iowa has been a leader in the development of rail-trails. Most conservation and recreation projects are conducted at the local level with a County Board of Conservation. Only one trail described here is managed by the Iowa Department of Natural Resources, although several county trails were established with the assistance of the DNR. Iowa has about 40 rail-trails of which 14 are described here. Another 9 are mentioned.

Rail-Trails of Northern Iowa

Described Trails

Trail Number	Name
I1	Butler County Nature Trail
I2	Cedar Valley Nature Trail
I2-A	Evansdale Nature Trail
I3	Great Lakes Spine Trail
I4	Harry Cook Nature Trail
I5	Heritage Trail
I6	Pony Hollow Trail
I6-A	Elkader River Walk
I7	Prairie Farmer Recreational Trail
I8	Puddle Jumper Trail
I9	Three Rivers Trail
I9-A	Gotch Spur
I10	Yellow River Forest Trail
I10-A	Allamakee County Conservation Board

Additional Trails

Trail Number	Name
I-A	Cedar Prairie Trail
I-B	Fort Dodge Nature Trail
I-C	Sergeant Road Trail
I-D	South Riverside Trail
I-E	Trolley / 218 Trail
I-F	Rockford Fossil & Prairie Park Trail
I-G	Wapsi - Great Western Line
I-H	Winkel Memorial Trail
I-I	Winnebago River Trail

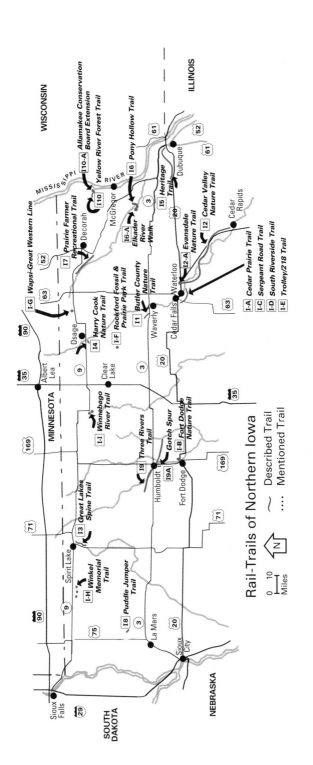

Rail-Trails of Northern Iowa

~ Described Trail

···· Mentioned Trail

0   10
Miles

N

WISCONSIN

ILLINOIS

MINNESOTA

SOUTH DAKOTA

NEBRASKA

MISSISSIPPI RIVER

10-A **Allamakee Conservation Board Extension**

10 **Yellow River Forest Trail**

16 **Pony Hollow Trail**

17 **Prairie Farmer Recreational Trail**

I-G **Wapsi-Great Western Line**

6-A **Elkader River Walk**

15 **Heritage Trail**

12 **Cedar Valley Nature Trail**

12-A **Evansdale Nature Trail**

11 **Butler County Nature Trail**

14 **Harry Cook Nature Trail**

I-F **Rockford Fossil & Prairie Park Trail**

I-A **Cedar Prairie Trail**
I-C **Sergeant Road Trail**
I-D **South Riverside Trail**
I-E **Trolley/218 Trail**

I-I **Winnebago River Trail**

19 **Three Rivers Trail**

19A **Gotch Spur**

I-B **Fort Dodge Nature Trail**

13 **Great Lakes Spine Trail**

I-H **Winkel Memorial Trail**

18 **Puddle Jumper Trail**

Decorah

McGregor

Dubuque

Cedar Rapids

Waterloo

Cedar Falls

Waverly

Osage

Clear Lake

Albert Lea

Humboldt

Fort Dodge

Spirit Lake

La Mars

Sioux City

Sioux Falls

52

63

90

35

169

71

9

3

20

35

169

71

75

3

20

9

90

29

61

61

52

20

63

11 Butler County Nature Trail

Butler County Conservation Board
Primary: Crushed rock. 🚶 🚴 ♿ ♿
FYI: There is a "Pack it in-pack it out" policy.
Length: 5.4 miles.
Fee: None.
Recommendation: It's short, so try it all.
FMI: Butler County Conservation Board
      28727 Timber Road
      Clarksville, IA 50619
      319-278-4237

General Trail Character: The Butler County Nature
Trail is well maintained. Nearly connecting two small
and spirited towns, it travels parallel to the Shell Rock
River through a rolling, lightly wooded landscape.
Like many Midwestern railroad lines, this one went
through several ownerships before its demise in the
late 1980's as part of the Chicago North Western Railroad system. Begun in 1871 by the Iowa-Pacific Railroad company, it was completed to Waverly in 1874.
In 1978 the line was taken over by the Dubuque and
Dakota Railroad Company, then sold to Butler
County in 1989. Some railroad era concrete mileage
markers still remain silently indicating the number of
miles to Chicago (about 280).

SHELL ROCK (to north end 5.4 miles)
On County Road T63, .3 mile north of State
Highway 3. 🚗 ⛱

Views along Butler County Nature Trail are dominated by farmsteads, fields, and woods. Along with
this comes prairie remnants and common rural wildlife. The trail doesn't quite make it to Clarksville, as
the tracks there are still active. About one mile from
Shell Rock a concrete-products factory interrupts the
right-of-way for a few hundred feet, but you can get
through. Probably the nicest one-mile section is
between Vail Avenue and 202nd Street, which offers a
comfortable mix of shade, longer views, prairie plants,
and the other pleasing elements of the Iowa landscape.

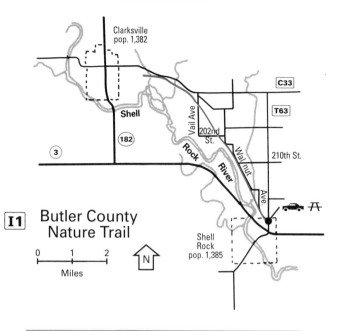

Butler County Nature Trail

I1

0 1 2
Miles
N

Clarksville pop. 1,382

Shell

C33

T63

Vail Ave

202nd St.

Walnut

210th St.

Rock River

3

182

Shell Rock pop. 1,385

Ave.

I2 Cedar Valley Nature Trail

Includes **Evansdale Nature Trail** (I2A)
Black Hawk and Linn County Conservation
Boards
Primary: Crushed rock.
FYI: A 10′ wide asphalt surface is planned for
Gilbertville to Evansdale in late spring, 1996.
Length: 52 miles.
Fee: Daily: $2.00 (age 16+).
Annual Pass: $8.00 (age 16+).
There are self-purchase stations along the trail.
Recommendation: Try La Porte to Brandon
(11 miles) or vice versa. For hiking start at
McFarlane Park then east toward Buzzards
Glory Quarry (3.5 miles).
FMI: Black Hawk County Conservation Board
        2410 W. Lone Tree Road
        Cedar Falls, IA 50613
        319-266-0328

        Waterloo Convention and Visitors
        Bureau
        215 E. 4th Street
        Waterloo, IA 50703
        319-233-8431

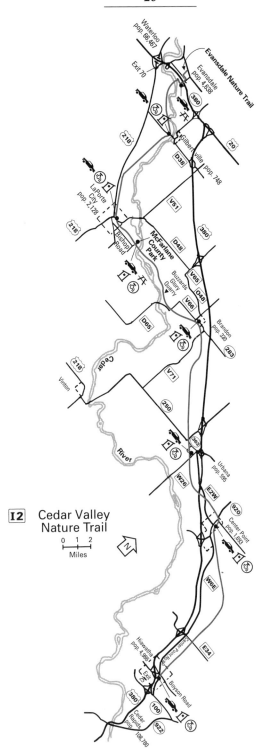

I2 Cedar Valley
Nature Trail

0 1 2
Miles

General Trail Character: Cedar Valley Nature Trail, one of Iowa's better trails, is advertised as the longest trail in the country that links two major metropolitan areas. It connects through the Cedar River valley, crossing the river twice. The Illinois Central Gulf Railroad abandoned this stretch of 52 miles, and one of their predecessors, the Waterloo, Cedar Falls, and Northern Interurban Railway, operated passenger service. Two of the depots used remain and have been restored. The railroad gave up in 1977, and the Cedar Valley Nature Trail opened late 1984. Private funds played a significant role in accomplishing this project.

> **HIAWATHA *(to Center Point, 13 miles; to Urbana, 5 miles; to Brandon, 9 miles)*****
> **Hiawatha:** I-380 exit 25, go east past Center Point Road (W6E) to access. 🚗 🚻
> **Center Point:** Along Franklin Street (old Depot area). 🚗 🚻 ♿
> **Urbana:** One block south of 363 near Brush Avenue. 🚗 🚻 ♿

The pleasant Iowa rural scenery starts almost immediately beyond the Hiawatha access. Be anxious to get to Center Point to view the restored depot. The open landscape continues to Urbana. The trail's diagonal route to Brandon parallels I-380 but at some distance.

> **BRANDON *(to McFarlane County Park, 6 miles; Park to La Porte City, 4 miles)*****
> **Brandon:** South side of town, off of Line Street. 🚗 🚻 ♿
> **McFarlane County Park:** Right in front of Park entrance. 🚗 🚻 ♿

If you look carefully 2.5 miles west of Brandon (between mile markers 22 and 23), you will see where the trail cuts through an ancient sand-dune ridge. Expect to see more woods and wildlife now as the trail crosses the broad Cedar River valley. Between Brandon and McFarlane County Park bald eagles have nested since 1993, the first known in Black Hawk County in over 100 years.

LA PORTE CITY *(to Gilbertville, 8 miles; to Evansdale, 5 miles)*
La Porte City: North side of town, along County Road D48. �

Gilbertville: West side of town, at Depot. 🚌 🏛 ♿

Evansdale: I-380 Exit 70 (River Forest Road). North on River Forest to Gilbert Drive, then east on Gilbert to Grand Boulevard. Right on Grand to Trail. Signs along the way will help. 🚌 🏕

From La Porte to Gilbertville you will parallel active tracks, Highway 218, and again be immersed in a rich agricultural landscape. At Gilbertville is a beautifully restored depot, which doubles as an access. The run to Evansdale offers occasional glimpses of oxbow wetlands (reminders that rivers meander over time), and the wide, flat, shallow river valley formed by glacial meltwaters is perfect for farms and trails. The finale is an impressive concrete arch bridge over the Cedar River. Here you take a short street detour to connect with the Evansdale Nature Trail.

Something Unique: Cedar Valley Nature Trail has a series of concerts at Buzzards Glory Quarry the second Saturday of June, July, and September. Hiking or biking to the site east of La Porte City is necessary, with trail rangers shuttling your belongings. A program fee is required. For information send 50 cents (cash or stamps) to: Cedar Trails Concert Series, Hartman Reserve Nature Center, 657 Reserve Drive, Cedar Falls, IA 50613.

More Trail: The **Evansdale Nature Trail** offers another mile of rail-trail from the north end of the Cedar Valley to Lafayette Street.

I3 Great Lakes Spine Trail

Dickinson County Conservation Board
Primary: Asphalt. 🏃 🚲 🛶 ♿ 🛷 🐴 (some portions)
Length: 10 miles.
Fees: None, but donation boxes are located along the trail.
Recommendation: If you want to see towns and lakes, stay in the center third. For a little bit of country, head to the north end.
FMI: Dickinson County Conservation Board
 1013 Okoboji Avenue
 Milford, Iowa 51355
 712-338-4786

 Iowa Great Lakes Area Chamber of Commerce
 Box 9
 Arnolds Park, IA 51331
 712-332-2107

General Trail Character: The Spine Trail is aptly named as it connects communities occupying the banks of the areas chain of lakes. You will probably see more water on this trail then even in Minnesota's north country. Here you experience a little bit of almost everything Iowa has to offer. While not all on a railroad, most of the trail does occupy a former Chicago, Milwaukee, St. Paul and Pacific route. Acquisition for trail purposes began in 1975 by the Iowa Department of Natural Resources, and ownership eventually ended up with the County Board. When not on the right-of-way, the trail creatively wanders through wildlife areas, parks, neighborhoods, and along Highway 71.

MILFORD (to Arnolds Park, 1.75 miles)
Milford: Exit U. S. Highway 71 east on 13th Street (A34), go 2 blocks. 🚗

From Milford to the Arnolds Park access is a mixed landscape of residential, field, and light industry. The trail is flat and well maintained. From the access south is another mile of trail, but it is primarily of local interest.

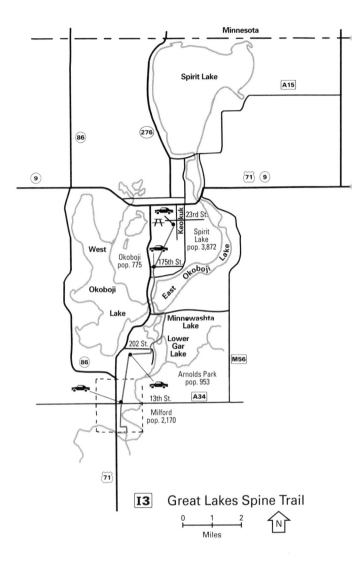

I3 Great Lakes Spine Trail

0   1   2
Miles

N

ARNOLDS PARK (to Okoboji, 5 miles)
Arnolds Park: Exit Highway 71 east on 202nd Street, go 3 blocks. 🚲

At the Arnolds Park access you head east on 202nd Street, using the well-marked paved shoulders. In about a mile you arrive at Lower Gar State Park, where things really get interesting. The trail now twists and turns along Lower Gar and Minnewashta Lakes, complete with a arched bridge over the connecting channel. Soon thereafter marked city streets continue the experience north. Be sure to linger at the trails midpoint bridge over the narrows separating East and West Lake Okoboji. With marinas on both sides and stairways to lower fishing platforms, there is always something to do or watch. Next are more neighborhoods and a stretch tight along Highway 71.

OKOBOJI (to Spirit Lake, 2.25 miles)
Okoboji: Exit Highway 71 east on 175th Street, go to 235th Avenue. 🚲

This northern stretch to the end at Spirit Lake abruptly leaves the lakes and neighborhood behind and heads diagonally through the rural landscape, gently shaded along the way. Stopping just a few blocks short of Highway 71 and the Dickinson County Historical Museum, this brings to a close a constantly changing 10-mile trail.

SPIRIT LAKE
Spirit Lake: West side of town. Exit Highway 71 south on Keokuk Avenue, go to 23rd Street and look for access. 🚲 🚻

Something Unique: West Okoboji Lake has been classified as one of the worlds few blue water lakes. Located on almost the highest point in Iowa there is little surface runoff into the lake and its waters are fed by springs. Enjoy this treasure at the mid-point bridge.

More Trail: Dozens of miles of local roads are advertised as bike routes. Maps are available locally.

14 Harry Cook Nature Trail
City of Osage
Primary: Crushed rock. 🚶 🚴 🛼 ⛷
FYI: With barricades and bumps, the trail is a little hard to negotiate by bicycle, but possible.
Length: 2 miles.
Fee: None.
Recommendation: Do it all if you can. Otherwise try the Spring Park end first.
FMI: Osage Parks and Recreation Department
114 South 7th Street
Osage, IA 50461
515-732-3709

Osage Chamber of Commerce
P. O. Box 305
Osage, IA 50461
515-732-3163

General Trail Character: The late William "Harry" Cook, a former Osage Park Board member, advocated connecting his city with the 47-acre Spring Park two miles west of town. This trail now does that. What made this possible was the availability of the Chicago Great Western Railway Company right-of-way, purchased by the City of Osage in 1961. Built by the Winona and Southwestern Railway Company in 1894, it was abandoned about 1900. Since then the right-of-way has been used as a walking path to Spring Park. Today it has been rediscovered and labeled a successful rail-trail.

OSAGE (to Spring Park, 2 miles)
Osage: On west side of town. From State Highway 9 take 1st Street South and go .4 mile to access on west side of road. 🚗

Harry Cook Nature Trail is best experienced by walking. What to enjoy here is subtle and gentle. Not far from the parking lot you begin to sense the antiquity of the abandonment, as in places erosion has removed it. Detours are provided, maintaining a continuous route, complete with a surprising amount of scenery, much of it wooded. The rest area with its scenic vista provides an elevated view of the Cedar River and should not be missed. The western .5 mile is very close to the river in a scenic, well-defined wooded valley. Hardwood forest species provide the canopy.

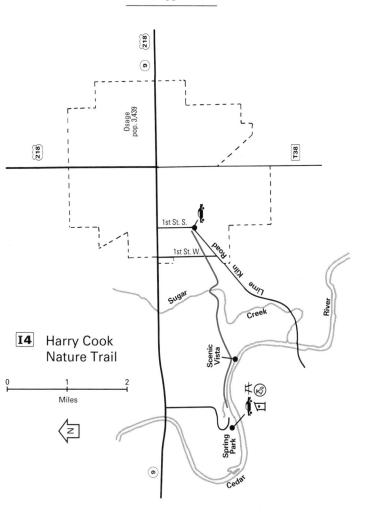

I4 Harry Cook Nature Trail

SPRING PARK

Spring Park: 1.5 miles west of town on Highway 9, then south at signs. 🚗 ⛱ 🏚 ♿

Spring Park is a beautiful oasis. The flowing spring (the information board says you can drink from it) and the resultant stream beg for exploration. If anywhere near Osage, swing by and enjoy this place.

Something Unique: In 1900 Mr. Price V. Evans, an Osage school principal, was murdered on the trail. The crime remains unsolved.

15 Heritage Trail

Dubuque County Conservation Board
Primary: Crushed rock. 🎿 🚲 ♿ (better
between Graf and Dubuque) ⚓
Length: 26 miles
Fees: $1.10 per day or $5.25 per year for
  ages 12–64.
  $0.60 per day or $2.75 per year for age 65
  and over.
Available at trail-side self-purchase stations.
Recommendation: Try Durango to Graf
(8 miles). If you can do more, continue west
to Kidder.
FMI: Dubuque County Conservation Board
  13768 Swiss Valley Road
  Peosta, IA 52068
  319-556-6745

  Dubuque Chamber of Commerce
  770 Main Street
  Dubuque, IA 52001
  319-557-9200
  800-255-2255 ext. 9200

General Trail Character: The Heritage Trail is perfectly
named, as it immerses you into a culturally rich and
dramatic landscape. This former Chicago to St. Paul
main line of the Chicago Great Western Railroad was
once nicknamed the "mountain railroad in a prairie
country," which helps explain the bluff and valley terrain traveled here. Railroad-era mileage markers still
exist and denote the distance from St. Paul (S) and
Chicago (C). Grain, timber, and lead ore were the
principal commodities hauled from the first days in
1886. Passenger service ended in 1956, with abandonment following in the 1970's. Scenically the trail
reflects two landscape types, with the transition being
near Farley. To the west is glaciated prairie, and to the
east is a driftless area of wooded bluffs and streams.

SAGEVILLE (to Graf, 12 miles)
Sageville: North of Dubuque two miles on
U. S. Highway 52. Look for signs. �car 🏛
Durango: Behind Trailside Cafe. 🚗 ♿

When trails parallel rivers, you are going either up or down. When leaving the Dubuque access, you are gently climbing and will to almost the very end, 470 vertical feet in all. Durango was once a lead-mining boom town, starting in 1836. Now it offers the only restaurant along the trail. The scenery gets better and better along the way to Graf. You will pass by quarry sites and traverse the towers of Split Rock. The wooded bluffs and floodplain forest provide plenty of shade. You can calculate your travel distance using the mileage markers provided along the way.

GRAF (to Farley, 8 miles)
Graf: Center of town at City Park. 🚗 🏕 🍴 ♿
Epworth (Kidder): North of town 2 miles along 1st Avenue NE, which becomes Gun Club Road (Y17). 🚗 🏕

Graf was a major train coal and water depot. Be sure to visit the road rock cut .3 mile west of the City Park and just across the road from the trail. Here you will find thousands of cephalopod fossils — no one seems to mind if you take a few. Moving on, you are never far from trout streams or the Little Maquoketa River. The Kidder access was once a railroad stop named for a local resident. The station here closed in 1928, but the site now makes a pleasant access. Your climb out of the valley is nearly over once you reach Farley.

FARLEY (to Dyersville, 6 miles)
Farley: On County Road Y13, .75 mile north of town. No facilities. Park in town, or on west side of Y13. 🚗
Dyersville: North side of town. From intersection of State Highway 136 and active railroad tracks, go east .5 mile on Heritage Trail Road to trail. 🚗

At Farley the 470-foot ascent from the Mississippi River is obviously over as you now level out and enter a glaciated prairie landscape. Farley itself has the usual 2 block downtown, which seems to be required of Iowa's small towns. From there to Dyersville (of *Field of Dreams* movie fame) the trail is on higher, open ground, paralleling active tracks. Remnant prairie pieces survive along the trail.

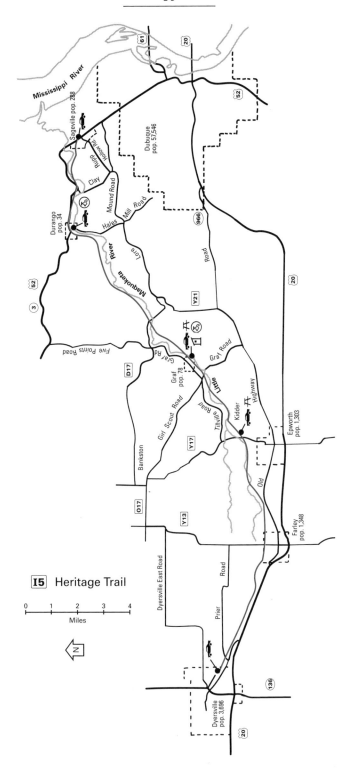

I5 Heritage Trail

0 1 2 3 4
Miles

N

Something Unique: Between Kidder and Graf is the virtually nonexistent town of Lattnerville. Here stands a stone church, visible from the trail and worth a sprint up the hill.

More Trail: Construction of a three mile extension from Sageville into the city limits of Dubuque is scheduled to begin Spring, 1996. Additional amenities of interest to trail visitors are under development at the Heritage Pond Wetland Park near Sageville.

16 Pony Hollow Trail

Includes Elkader River Walk (16-A)
Clayton County Conservation Board
Primary: Natural 🚶 🚲 ⛷ 🐎
Length: 4 miles.
Fees: None.
Recommendation: If walking, try to do it all and arrange for someone to pick you up at one end or the other. If biking, you could complete the loop using either High Street or Highway 13.
FMI: Clayton County Conservation Board
    Osborne Center
    29862 Osborne Road
    Elkader, IA 52043
    319-245-1516

    Elkader Area Chamber of Commerce
    918 High Street North East
    Elkader, IA 52043
    319-245-2372

General Trail Character: The Pony Hollow Trail may be Iowa's best-kept rail-trail secret. Elkader and this trail could become a major draw, as they have the ingredients of scenery, history, and mystery. The old and minimally maintained right-of-way is fascinating if you like to discover places and things on your own. This grade began in 1872 as the Iowa Eastern from Beulah Junction north of town and followed a tortuous route. It ended as part of the Milwaukee Road in the early 1970's. On the way south it paralleled Roberts / Pony Hollow Creeks to the Turkey River, then west along the river to the south side of Elkader

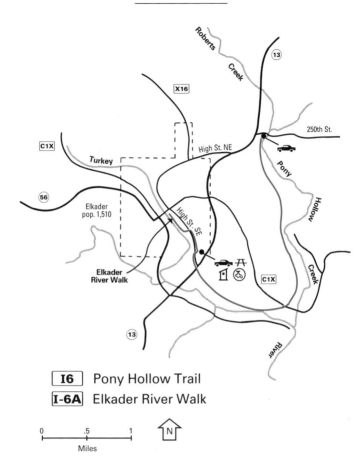

I6 Pony Hollow Trail
I-6A Elkader River Walk

0   .5   1
Miles

where it turned north into town. This practically created a loop, which is unique to rail-trails in the upper
Midwest. It offers exposure to tight valleys, wooded
slopes, floodplain forests, and small farms.

ELKADER South (to north access, 4 miles)
Elkader City Park, south side of town near the
intersection of State Highway 13 and High
Street SE. Follow the mowed path on the west
side of High Street south, under the Highway
13 bridge, to the trail.

At the City Park access is a caboose, left as a tribute to
the contribution the railroad made to the community.
Once on the mowed path past Highway 13, in just
a few hundred feet you will feel close and involved

with this hidden valley landscape. The curving route creates even more interest as you constantly wonder what's ahead. At about the trail's midpoint you leave the Turkey River valley and in a broad curve head up the Pony Hollow Creek valley (no one seems to know why it's named that). Expect to find a downed tree, rough spot, or washout. The trail is regularly used by horses.

ELKADER North

Elkader (north): Leave Elkader on Highway 13 north, go to 250th Street, then east 1 block to trail on right. �car
Between the two accesses is the County Road C1X crossing.

Something Unique: Don't miss Elkader's historic downtown district. Spanning the Turkey River is the 346 foot long Keystone Bridge, completed in 1889. The Keystone Restaurant has a patio along the river with nice views of the bridge.

More Trail: The City Park access is connected to downtown by the **Elkader River Walk** which is probably more of the same right-of-way. A walking tour brochure is available locally.

I7 Prairie Farmer Recreational Trail

Winneshiek County Conservation Board
Primary: Crushed rock. 🏃 🚲 🏇 ♿ 🎣
(Ridgeway to Cresco)
Length: 17 miles.
Fees: None.
Recommendation: Try Calmar to Conover and slightly beyond (4 miles).
FMI: Winneshiek County Conservation Board
    2546 Lake Meyer Road
    Ft. Atkinson, IA 52144
    319-534-7145

    Calmar Tourism Committee
    c/o City Clerk
    201 North Maryville
    Calmar, IA 52132
    319-562-3154

General Trail Character: Finally, a trail named after the most common neighbor of upper Midwest trails. It's about time this happened. Occupying a high prairie ridge, the trail offers exactly what it advertises—fresh air and open spaces. The line got started in 1866 as the McGregor Western, connecting McGregor to Cresco. Tapping into the rich agricultural harvests was the major motivator. Only a year later it became part of the Milwaukee and St. Paul Railroad, which covered much of southern Wisconsin and Iowa. The name was changed in 1874 to the Chicago, Milwaukee and St. Paul, more commonly known as the Milwaukee Road.

CALMAR (to Ridgeway, 12 miles)
Calmar: Downtown at the intersection of U. S Highway 52 and the active railroad tracks, next to the old depot. Signed from Highway 52. 🚗

For a short distance out of Calmar the railroad history is obvious as the trail parallels active tracks. They then split as the trail takes the high ridge toward Cresco. The more wooded and sheltered portions of trail are found near Conover (pop. 10?) after which you emerge into the open agricultural landscape. Now only occasionally wooded, grass, and prairie species dominate.

RIDGEWAY (toward Cresco, 5 miles)
Ridgeway: Ridgeway Roadside Park, along State Highway 9 on south side of town.
🚗 ⛱ 🚻 ♿

Ridgeway offers a nice park for trail and highway users. A convenient and signed city-street detour takes you through town since the right-of-way was converted to commercial development. Prairie Farmer closely parallels Highway 9 as it finishes the run toward Cresco. Mileage markers, which start at Calmar, keep you informed of your progress.

CRESCO
Cresco: 2 miles east of town along Highway 9 at 345th Avenue. 🚗

Something Unique: The trail misses Spillville by 3 miles where you find the famous clock museum. In Cresco a Milwaukee Road engine and caboose are on display at a downtown City Park.

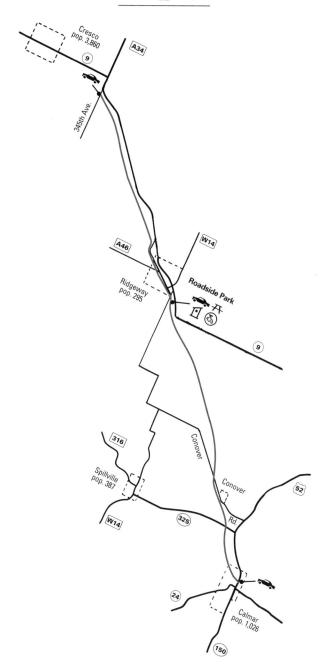

17 Prairie Farmer Recreational Trail

0   1   2
Miles

18 Puddle Jumper Trail

City of Orange City
Primary: Crushed rock. 🚶 🚲 🛼 ♿
Secondary: Natural. 🐎
Length: 2.3 miles.
Fees: None.
Recommendation: It's short, so try it all.
Otherwise start at the mid point access and
go east to the lookout platforms (.5 mile).
FMI: City Hall
125 Central Avenue Southeast
Orange City, IA 51041
712-737-4885

Orange City Chamber of Commerce
125 Central Avenue Southeast
P. O. Box 36
Orange City, IA 51041
712-737-4510

General Trail Character: Everything about this trail was
done well and with a little wit such as naming the trail
Puddle Jumper. The accesses are well designed, attractive places to linger and enjoy. The trail also offers
something no other Midwest trail does: bison (buffalo).
About a dozen or so can be seen from short lookout
platforms .5 mile east of the midpoint access. Orange
City is the home of Northwestern College, and profes-
sors there have been planting native prairie grasses
and forbs along this former Chicago and North Western right-of-way. This makes for a better understand-
ing of the bison/prairie ecological connection that
once existed. Some very light woods and shrub areas
provide accent in this otherwise open environment.

ORANGE CITY (to Alton, 2.3 miles)
Orange City: South side of town. Exit State
Highway 10 south on County Road K64, go
two blocks (directly across street from Vogel
Paints). 🚗 🍽
Mid Point: East of Orange City about 1 mile.
Exit Highway 10 south on Jay Avenue, go two
blocks. 🚗 🍽 🏛

You know you are somewhere a little bit different
when a huge Dutch windmill marks the trail's gateway from Orange City. The secondary trail is labeled

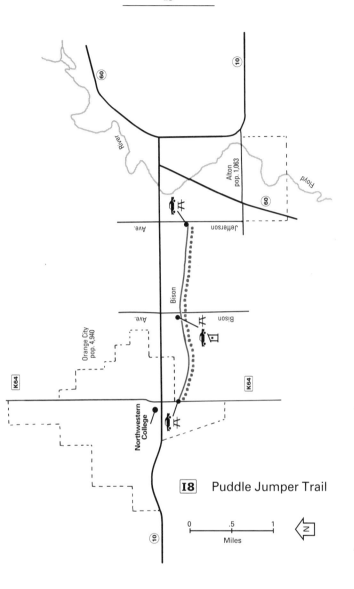

18 Puddle Jumper Trail

0 — .5 — 1
Miles

N

"Bridal Path." While you may not be tired by the time
you get to the midpoint access only a mile away it's
such a pleasant spot you might as well try it. In just
another .5 mile the bison are on the north side. Use
the lookout platforms, but please remember that these
fenced-in critters are not pets and should not be fed or
teased. Bring your camera.

ALTON
Alton: West side of town. Exit Highway 10
south on Jefferson Avenue, go three blocks.

Something Unique: The bison, of course. In addition,
Orange City is primarily of Dutch ancestry, and you
see the evidence everywhere. Even the local chamber
of commerce brochure says, "Breng ons een bezoek"
(Pay us a visit). Good advice.

19 Three Rivers Trail and Gotch Spur (19-A)

Humboldt, Pocahontas, Wright County
Conservation Boards
Primary: Crushed rock.
FYI: Trail development in progress at each of
the three ends.
Length: Three Rivers: 32 miles.
          Gotch Spur: 3 miles.
Fees: None.
Recommendation: From Dakota City try the
Gotch Spur south or the Three Rivers east.
From Bradgate west is also good. For longer
experiences braving the open areas is necessary.
FMI: Humboldt County Conservation Board
        Courthouse
        Dakota City, IA 50529
        515-332-4087

        Humboldt–Dakota City Chamber of
        Commerce
        29 5th Street South
        P. O. Box 247
        Humboldt, IA 50548
        515-332-1481

General Trail Character: The Three Rivers Trail and
Gotch Spur are ambitious projects that travel a river-
dissected prairie landscape, crossing the West and
East Branch of the Des Moines River. Two railroad
lines are involved. Three Rivers occupies the Chicago
and North Western Railroad for 32 miles, while the
Gotch Spur took possession of the Minneapolis and
St. Louis Line. There are 28 renovated trestles. The

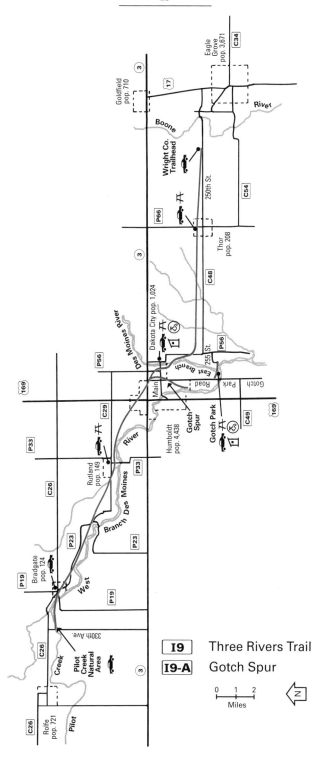

Eagle Grove pop. 3,671

C34

Goldfield pop. 710

3

17

Boone River

Wright Co. Trailhead

250th St.

C54

P66

3

C48

Thor pop. 208

Des Moines River

Dakota City pop. 1,024

255 St.

P56

Gotch Park Road

P56

East Branch

Gotch River

169

C49

Gotch Park

169

C29

P33

River

Humboldt pop. 4,438

Gotch Spur

Main

Rutland pop. 149

C26

P33

P23

Branch Des Moines

P23

Bradgate pop. 124

West

P19

P19

330th Ave.

C26

Creek

Pilot Creek Natural Area

3

C26

Rolfe pop. 721

Pilot

I9 Three Rivers Trail

I9-A Gotch Spur

0 1 2
Miles

N

character of these trails changes abruptly and more than once, ranging from well-wooded and intimate to wide, wide open. Very small towns with few services (except Humboldt and Dakota City) offer some off-trail exploration opportunities.

Three Rivers Trail

ROLFE (to Bradgate, 4 miles)
Rolfe: Trail not complete into town yet. Use next access.
Pilot Creek Natural Area: West of Bradgate. From County Road C26 turn south on 330th Avenue. Trail is in .5 mile and parking area is 100 yards farther on the east side of road. ➡

From east of Rolfe to Bradgate you will experience an intimate, well-wooded, sheltered valley hidden from the surrounding landscape. It comes as quite a shock when compared to the surrounding openness. This valley soon joins with the West Branch Des Moines River and its forested floodplain. A long bridge takes you over the river. By now you will also have passed the Sterns Woods Natural Area.

BRADGATE (to Dakota City, 14 miles)
Bradgate: Street parking most anywhere. There is a City Park on the east side of town on County Road C26. ➡
Rutland: City Park. From C29 go south on 2nd Street one block. ➡ ⊓
Humboldt: Use Dakota City Access. ➡

After Bradgate, while still in the river valley, the views open up considerably and agriculture dominates. Now only occasionally wooded and visited by parallel roads, the trail passes below the grain elevators in Rutland, then later skim the north side of Humboldt. Through Humboldt the woods pick up again, you cross Highway 3, intersect with the Gotch Spur, and by Dakota City the scenic East Branch Des Moines River valley takes over.

DAKOTA CITY (to Wright County Trailhead, 14 miles)
Dakota City: Highway 3 / trail crossing. ➡
Dakota City: Ricer Park, east side of town. Along the north side of County Road P56

between trail and East Fork Des Moines River.
P56 enters town at the intersection of 1st
Avenue North and 8th Street. 🚗 🏕 🏪
Thor: City Park on north side of town. 🚗 🏕

Perched on a terrace between river and ridge, the trail
continues a mile or so from Ricer Park to another impressive river crossing. Enjoy the views and shade, as
now the valley is left behind. All the way to the Wright
County Trailhead is as straight and open as a trail can
get. Native prairie plant species are common in the
right-of-way. Thor, despite being mostly boarded up,
is a welcome interruption.

Wright County Trailhead
East of Thor 4 miles along 250th Street. 🚗
A trail extension into Eagle Grove is planned
for 1995.

Gotch Spur (I9-A)

DAKOTA CITY (south, 2 miles)
Dakota City: East of downtown, where Main
Street crosses the trail. Street parking. 🚗

The Gotch Spur takes you south out of town via the
West Fork Des Moines River valley, offering shade
and wildlife sightings. Unfortunately the route to
Gotch Park is not yet secured, and getting through is
not possible.

GOTCH PARK (to 255th Street, 1 mile)
Gotch Park: 3 miles south of Dakota City on
Gotch Park Road. 🚗 🏕 🏪 ♿

The trail passes through this wooded park, which
offers camping, river access, picnic shelter, and more.
Once through the park, you cross the East Branch Des
Moines River but then soon run out of trail at 255th
Street, a remote road next to a defunct power plant.

Something Unique: Along Gotch Spur in Dakota City
(at the Main Street crossing) is a privately owned,
large, and colorful caboose with a passenger car from
the Illinois Central Railroad.

110 Yellow River Forest Trail

Includes Allamakee County Conservation
Board Extension (110-A)
Iowa Department of Natural Resources
Allamakee County Conservation Board
Primary: Natural 🚶 🚲 👟 🐎 🐕

FYI: This is Iowa's most rugged and wild
place. The trail is minimally developed.
The Allamakee County Conservation Board
recently secured another 1.5 miles of right-of-
way to extend the trail to Waukon Junction.

Length: 5 miles

Fees: None (except for camping).

Recommendation: Head out from the access in
either direction. Going upstream, the trail is
wooded and constricted. Downstream you get
better views of the bluffs.

FMI: Yellow River State Forest
729 State Forest Road
Harpers Ferry, IA 52146
319-586-2254

Allamakee County Tourism and
Economic Development Commission
110 Allamakee Street
Waukon, IA 52172
319-568-2624
800-824-1424

General Trail Character: The Yellow River State Forest–
Paint Creek Unit is 4,500 acres of public land in the
heart of Iowa's bluffland country. The dramatic
scenery cannot be exaggerated. The 1.5 miles of trail
from the Paint Creek Unit to Waukon Junction is on
privately owned portions of right-of-way, but easements for public use were secured by the Conservation
Board. Deep valleys such as Paint Creek offered the
only routes for the railroad to escape the Mississippi
valley. This one began in 1877 as the 3-foot narrow-
gauge Waukon and Mississippi Railroad connecting
Waukon Junction on the river to Waukon 23 miles
away. It ended up as part of the Milwaukee Road system in 1880 and was converted to standard gauge in
1884. Grain was the cargo, but at the turn of the century iron ore was hauled from Iron Hill. This geologi-

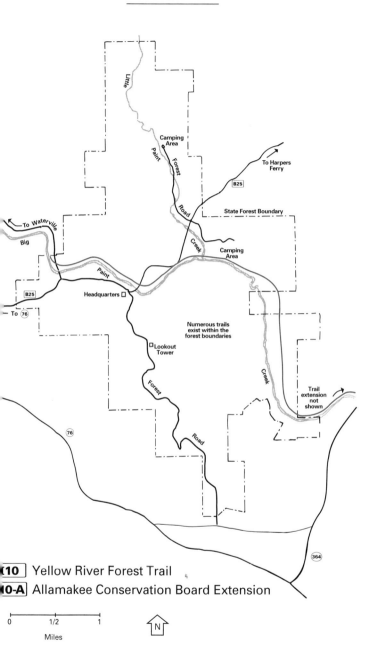

(10) Yellow River Forest Trail

(10-A) Allamakee Conservation Board Extension

Labels within the map:
Little
Paint
Forest
Road
Camping Area
B25
To Harpers Ferry
State Forest Boundary
To Waterville
Big
Paint
Creek
Camping Area
B25
To 76
Headquarters
Numerous trails exist within the forest boundaries
Lookout Tower
Forest
Creek
Trail extension not shown
Road
76
364

0   1/2   1
Miles

N

cal freak, 2.5 miles north of Waukon, yielded high-grade ore and not surprisingly has been Iowa's only major iron mine. Difficult to maintain, the line was abandoned, and the right-of-way within the forests boundaries was purchased by the State of Iowa in 1971.

YELLOW RIVER STATE FOREST (to Waukon Junction, 5 miles)
Yellow River State Forest: Paint Creek Unit. From Marquette go 12 miles north on State Highway 76 to County Road X25 (State Forest Road), then east 2 mile to Unit. Access is on the right at Paint Creek bridge. ➤ ⚲ 🏕

The bluffs, woods, and Big Paint Creek at the access are typical of the qualities to be explored. The trail shadows this cold-water designated trout stream nearly the entire length. At times the route is wet but entirely negotiable. Views of 350-400 foot bluffs are common, turkeys are everywhere, and there are great displays of spring woodland wildflowers. Strenuous loop options with other hiking trails are possible. Minimally developed campsites are available, and some are specifically intended for equestrians.

Something Unique: Go off the trail to Waterville. It might remind you of a Ozark mountain town. Along the way look for the right-of-way with original iron bridges.

Iowa – Additional Rail-Trails

*The rail trails listed here may be short, primarily of local interest,
under development, or only a small part of a longer trail. They are
listed by management structure.*

CITY

I-A   Cedar Prairie Trail, Cedar Falls
Length: 4.5 total, 0.6 Rail-Trail
Surface: Concrete
Primary uses: 🏃 🚲
FMI: City of Cedar Falls
  Park Division
  606 Union Road
  Cedar Falls, IA 50613
  319-273-8624
Comments: Chicago and North Western right-of-way.
Connects to an extensive system of urban trails.

I-B   Fort Dodge Nature Trail, Fort Dodge
Length: 2.9 total, 2.9 Rail-Trail
Surface: Crushed rock
Primary uses: 🏃 🚲 🏇
FMI: Fort Dodge Parks Department
  819 First Avenue South
  Fort Dodge, IA 50501
  515-576-7237
Comments: Parallels Soldier Creek. Snell / Crawford is the
best access. The lower end is in a intimate, scenic valley.

I-C   Sergeant Road Trail, Waterloo
Length: 5.2 total, 5.2 Rail-Trail
Surface: Crushed rock
Primary uses: 🏃 🚲
FMI: Waterloo Parks Commission
  1101 Campbell Avenue
  Waterloo, IA 50701
  319-291-4370
Comments: Parallels Highway 63 (Sergeant Road).

I-D   South Riverside Trail, Cedar Falls
Length: 2.1 total, 2.1 Rail-Trail
Surface: Asphalt
Primary uses: 🏃 🚲 🏇
FMI: see Cedar Prairie Trail
Comments: Former Rock Island Railroad. Connects to the
Hartman Reserve and Pfeiffer Spring's Park.

I-E   Trolley / 218 Trail, Waterloo
Length: 2.0 total, 0.5 Rail-Trail
Surface: Natural & concrete
Primary uses: 🏃 🚲
FMI: see Sergeant Road Trail
Comments: A portion of this trail occupies an old trolley
right-of-way.

COUNTY

I-F **Rockford Fossil and Prairie Park, Rockford (west 1.5 miles)**
Length: 5.0 total, 1.0 Rail-Trail
Surface: Original ballast
Primary uses: 🚶 🏃
FMI: Floyd County Conservation Board
1958 Highway 18
Charles City, IA 50616
515-257-6214
Comments: Under development. The park is 50 acres of prairie and old quarry loaded with Devonian Period fossils.

I-G **Wapsi–Great Western Line, Riceville**
Length: 6.0 total, 4.0 Rail-Trail
Surface: Crushed rock
Primary uses: 🚶 🚴 🏃
FMI: Wapsi–Great Western Line Committee
P.O. Box 116
Riceville, IA 50466
515-985-4030
Comments: Contains maintained prairie and a butterfly garden. Travels through Lake Hendricks Park.

I-H **Winkel Memorial Trail, Sibley to Allendorf**
Length: 10.0 total, 6.0 Rail-Trail
Surface: Original ballast
Primary uses: 🚶 🚴 🐎 ⛷
FMI: Osceola County Conservation Board
5945 Highway 9
Ocheyedan, IA 51354
712-758-3709
Comments: Under development. Snowmobiling and skiing allowed after hunting season.

I-I **Winnebago River Trail, Forest City**
Length: 2.5 total, 2.5 Rail-Trail
Surface: Original ballast
Primary uses: 🚶 🚴
FMI: Winnebago County Conservation Board
34496 110th Avenue
Forest City, IA 50436
515-565-3390
Comments: Under development. Travels a shallow river valley. A 3.5 mile trail extension along state and county roads has been funded.

3:
Rails-Trails of Minnesota

Minnesotans love to visit trails, especially by bicycle and snowmobile. Over one half of the state's population lives in the Twin Cities metropolitan area, where dozens of miles of trails have been developed along the rivers and lakes. The trail bonanza has spread to the other urban centers and rural Minnesota. This chapter describes 24 trails, some of which are quite lengthy, and mentions 35 others. Many of the trails are administered by the Minnesota Department of Natural Resources through the Trails and Waterways, Forestry, or Parks and Recreation Divisions. To request information and maps from the DNR, use the following address and phone numbers:

Minnesota Department of Natural Resources
Information Center
500 Lafayette Road
St. Paul, MN 55155-4040

In the Twin Cities and Out of State: 612-296-6157
Within Minnesota: 1-800-766-6000
Telecommunications Device for the Deaf:
In the Twin Cities and Out of State: 612-296-5484
Within Minnesota: 1-800-657-3929

Information Center Hours:
Monday–Friday: 8:00 a.m. through 4:15 p.m. CST

Fees: When cross-country skiing on most public trails in Minnesota, you need a Great Minnesota Ski Pass if you are aged 16–64. Funds raised from the sale of ski passes are used for the improvement and maintenance of ski trails. They are available by mail and phone order from the Minnesota DNR Information Center as well as many retail outlets that typically sell hunting and fishing licenses. The 1996 costs are:

> Daily: $1.00
> Individual season: $5.00
> 3-year individual: $14.00
> Husband and wife season: $7.50
> 3-year husband and wife: $14.00

A 50-cent issuing fee may be added when purchasing from a retail outlet.

To enter a Minnesota State Park with a vehicle requires a vehicle-admission sticker, available from the Minnesota DNR Information Center and park-entrance stations. The 1996 costs are:

> Daily: $4.00
> Season: $18.00
> 2nd vehicle season: $12.00
> Senior / handicapped season: $12.00

Rail-Trails of Minnesota

Described Trails

Additional Trails

M-I	St. Croix Bikeway
M-J	Waterfront Promenade
M-K	West Mankato Trail
M-L	West River Parkway
M-M	Big Rivers Regional Trail
M-N	Burlington Northern Regional Trail
M-O	Hardwood Creek Trail
M-P	Red Jacket Trail
M-Q	Sunrise Prairie Trail
M-R	Mesabi Range Trail
M-S	Soo Line Trail, Northern Route
M-T	Soo Line Trail, Southern Route
M-U	Arrowhead State Trail
M-V	Banning State Park Quarry and Spur Trail
M-W	Blue Ox Trail
M-X	Casey Jones State Trail
M-Y	Circle L Trail
M-Z	Circle T Trail
M-AA	Cloquet to Saginaw
M-AB	Gandy Dancer Trail
M-AC	Goodhue–Pioneer Trail
M-AD	Minnehaha Trail
M-AE	Pengilly to Alborn
M-AF	Racine Prairie State Natural Area
M-AG	Shooting Star Prairie State Natural Area
M-AH	Taconite State Trail
M-AI	Wild Indigo State Natural Area

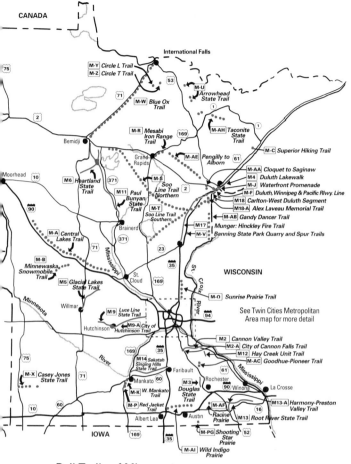

CANADA

International Falls

M-Y *Circle L Trail*
M-Z *Circle T Trail*

M-U *Arrowhead State Trail*

M-W *Blue Ox Trail*

M-R *Mesabi Iron Range Trail*

M-AH *Taconite State Trail*

Bemidji

M-AE *Pengilly to Alborn*

M-C *Superior Hiking Trail*

Grand Rapids

M6 *Heartland State Trail*

Moorhead

M-S *Soo Line Trail Northern*

M11 *Paul Bunyan State Trail*

M-AA *Cloquet to Saginaw*
M4 *Duluth Lakewalk*
M-J *Waterfront Promenade*
M-F *Duluth, Winnipeg & Pacific Rlwy. Line*
M18 *Carlton-West Duluth Segment*
M18-A *Alex Laveau Memorial Trail*
M-AB *Gandy Dancer Trail*

M-T *Soo Line Trail Southern*

Brainerd

M-A *Central Lakes Trail*

M-B *Minnewaska Snowmobile Trail*

M17 *Munger: Hinckley Fire Trail*
M-V *Banning State Park Quarry and Spur Trails*

M5 *Glacial Lakes State Trail*

St. Cloud

WISCONSIN

M-O *Sunrise Prairie Trail*

Willmar

See Twin Cities Metropolitan Area map for more detail

M9 *Luce Line State Trail*

M9-A *City of Hutchinson Trail*

Hutchinson

M2 *Cannon Valley Trail*
M2-A *City of Cannon Falls Trail*
M12 *Hay Creek Unit*
M-AC *Goodhue-Pioneer Trail*

M-X *Casey Jones State Trail*

M14 *Sakatah Singing Hills State Trail*

Faribault

M3 *Douglas State Trail*

Rochester

Winona

La Crosse

M13-A *Harmony-Preston Valley Trail*

Mankato

M-K *W. Mankato Trail*

M-P *Red Jacket Trail*

M-AF *Racine Prairie*

M13 *Root River State Trail*

Albert Lea

Austin

M-PG *Shooting Star Prairie*

M-AI *Wild Indigo Prairie*

IOWA

Rail Trails of Minnesota

Described Trail
••••• Mentioned Trail

0   5   10
Miles

N

Rail-Trails of the Twin Cities Metropolitan Area

Described

Trail Number	Name
M1	Afton State Park
	Hennepin Parks Southwest Regional Light Rail Transit Trails:
M7	Northern Route
M8	Southern Route
M8-A	City of Chanhassen Trail
M9	Luce Line State Trail
M9-A	City of Plymouth Trail
M10	Minnesota Valley Trail State Park
M15	Stone Arch Bridge
	Willard Munger State Trail:
M16	Gateway Trail Segment

Additional Trails

Trail Number	Name
M-D	Burlington Northern Regional Trail
M-E	Cedar Lake Trail
M-G	Loop Trail System
M-H	Midtown Greenway
M-I	St. Croix Bikeway
M-L	West River Parkway
M-M	Big Rivers Regional Trail
M-N	Burlington Northern Regional Trail
M-O	Hardwood Creek Trail
M-Q	Sunrise Prairie Trail
M-R	Mesabi Range Trail
M-S	Soo Line Trail, Northern Route
M-T	Soo Line Trail, Southern Route
M-AD	Minnehaha Trail

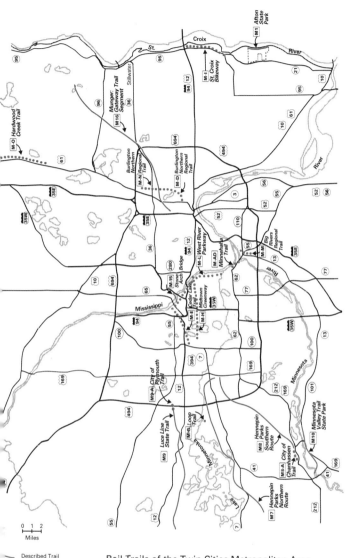

Rail Trails of the Twin Cities Metropolitan Area

Described Trail
Mentioned Trail

M1 Afton State Park

Minnesota Department of Natural Resources,
Parks and Recreation
Primary: Crushed rock. 🏃 ⛷ 🚲 (north half
only)
Length: 2.25 miles.
Fees: Vehicle entrance sticker, Great Minnesota
Ski Pass.
Recommendation: It's short, so try it all. If your
time is limited, do the south end first.
FMI: Afton State Park Manager
　　　6959 Peller Avenue South
　　　Hastings, MN 55033
　　　612-436-5391

　　　Hastings Area Chamber of Commerce
　　　1304 Vermillion Street
　　　Hastings, MN 55033
　　　612-437-6775

General Trail Character: Minimally developed, much of
the park's interior is accessible only by foot. The resources include deep forested ravines, trout streams,
prairie restoration areas, and over two miles of frontage
on the St. Croix River. Tight along the banks of the
federally designated wild and scenic St. Croix River is
the bed of this former Milwaukee railroad. It once
connected Stillwater and Hastings and was abandoned
in the 1970's. Had more of this route been converted
to trail, it would have been a place of national signifi-
cance. However, abandonments at that time were often
too early for successful conversion because of intense
adjacent landowner opposition, as was the case here.

AFTON STATE PARK

Park entrance is between Stillwater and Hastings, just south of Afton at the intersection
of County Roads 20 and 21. Well-marked.
🚗 🪧 🏚 ♿

Paralleling the St. Croix River, this trail offers stunning
views of the valley and river traffic. The route is sheltered and alive with birds, especially warblers in the
spring and migrating hawks and eagles in the fall. Try
the swimming beach if warm. The water quality is
excellent. Other park facilities include a visitor center

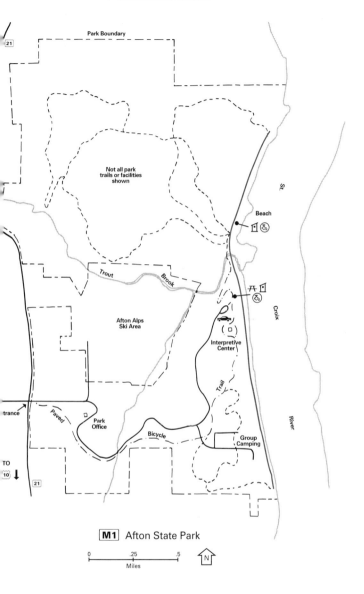

M1 Afton State Park

0   .25   .5

Miles

with interpretive displays, backpack-only camping areas, and miles of trail. The park virtually surrounds the private Afton Alps Ski Area.

More Trail: There are miles of excellent hiking trails in the park as well as some bicycle trails.

M2 Cannon Valley Trail

Includes **City of Cannon Falls Trail** M2-A
Joint Powers Board
City of Cannon Falls
Primary: Asphalt. 🚶 🚲 🛼 ⛷ ♿
FYI: No pets (even in baskets and trailers).
Length: 19.7 miles.
Fees: Wheel Pass for biking, in-line skating if age 18 or older. Available at self-purchase stations. The 1996 rates are: $2 per day or $10 per year. Great Minnesota Ski Pass.
Recommendation: Cannon Falls to Welch (9.5 miles) is highly recommended. If hiking, try from the westerly Sunset Trail (a township road) and the trail intersection back toward Cannon Falls. Get at least as far as the Anderson Rest Area (1 mile).
FMI: Cannon Valley Trail,
     306 West Mill Street
     Cannon Falls, MN 55009
     507-263-3954

     Cannon Falls Area Chamber of
     Commerce
     103 North Fourth Street
     Cannon Falls, MN 55009
     507-263-2289

General Trail Character: The Cannon Valley Trail was designed for a quiet, people-powered experience through the scenic lower Cannon River Valley. Diversity is what makes this trail special. This Minnesota Central Railroad line once connected Red Wing with Mankato, a distance of almost 100 miles, and later merged into the Chicago Great Western Railroad, which in 1968 became part of the Chicago North Western system. In 1983 the line from Red Wing to Cannon Falls was abandoned. Local citizens purchased the right-of-way and the trestles with donated funds, secured grants for development, and convinced the cities of Cannon Falls, Red Wing, and Goodhue County to manage the project with a joint powers board. Gently twisting and turning to stay parallel to the Cannon River, a designated wild and scenic river, the magnificent valley can be explored and enjoyed.

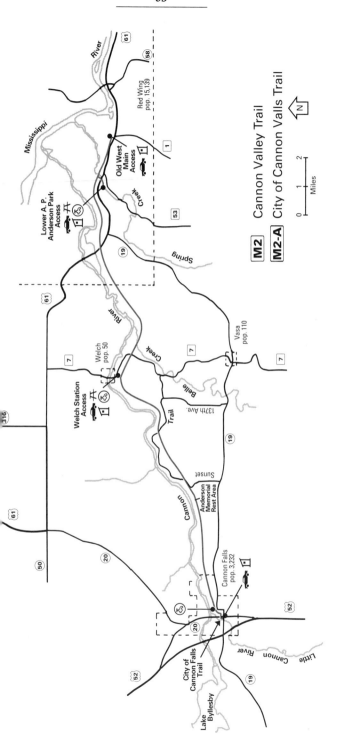

Cannon Valley Trail

City of Cannon Valls Trail

CANNON FALLS (to Welch, 9.5 miles)

Cannon Falls: via City Trail in downtown, on State Highway 19 one block west of stoplight. ⇢ 🏕

🍴 ♿ available within one mile

The Cannon Falls City Trail winds along both the Little Cannon and Cannon rivers before reaching the Cannon Valley Trail on the east side of town. When leaving Cannon Falls, almost immediately you enter an outstanding prairie-remnant area. This is abruptly followed by a gradual descent through north facing (and cool) rock cuts loaded with ferns, rare plants, and a view of the river 40 feet below. The Anderson Memorial Rest Area 3.5 miles out of town (use the mileage markers to keep track) is not to be missed. Here a small trout stream, picnic area, and river access trail combine to make a terrific place to linger. The trail's midpoint is called Welch Station Access and is another comfortable place to stop.

WELCH (to Red Wing, 10.2 miles)

Welch: .3 miles south of downtown Welch just off of County Boulevard 7. ⇢ 🍴 🏕 ♿

From Welch to Red Wing you'll first pass Welch Ski Village, then experience extensive forests and wild places, scenic views, and probably wild turkeys. The final mile is urban and ends just short of Red Wing's famous Pottery Shopping District. A signed bike route takes you to this historic place or to Bay Point Park along the Mississippi River one mile farther.

RED WING

Red Wing: Two accesses, both signed from Highway 61. Lower A. P. Anderson Park has all facilities. Old West Main Access is further into town (no water there). ⇢ 🍴 🏕 ♿

Something Unique: Visit Welch, a funky little village of 39 on the banks of the Cannon River, only .3 mile north of the trail at Welch Station Access. Look for signs on the trail.

More Trail: In Red Wing the trail is 1.5 miles short of the **Richard J. Dorer Memorial Hardwood State Forest Trail–Hay Creek Unit.** In Cannon Falls is the **City of Cannon Falls Trail,** two miles long.

M3 Douglas State Trail

Minnesota Department of Natural Resources,
Trails and Waterways
Primary: Asphalt. 👫 🚲 🛷 ♿ 🚣
Secondary: Natural. 🎿 🐎
Length: 12.5 miles.
Fees: Great Minnesota Ski Pass.
Recommendation: Pine Island to Douglas,
(8 miles) or vice versa.
FMI: DNR Information Center

> Rochester Area Chamber of Commerce
> 220 South Broadway, #100
> Rochester, MN 55904
> 507-288-1122

General Trail Character: The Douglas State Trail will
expose you to the gentle, agricultural scenery of
southern Minnesota with a touch of urban at the
Rochester end. This trail was once part of the extensive and proud Chicago Great Western Railway Company system. The iron bridges and occasional turn-
of-the-century mileage markers remind you of this
heritage. It is one of Minnesota's older rail-trails and
is popular with Rochester residents. By Minnesota
standards this is a short trail, and you can also expect
it to be busy at times. It is level and paved, easy for
families and a favorite with in-line skaters.

ROCHESTER (to Douglas, 4.5 miles)

Rochester: Exit U. S. Highway 52 at 55th
Street NW. Go west and south following
County Road 22 (West Circle Drive) to
County Road 4. Then east to access. 🚗 🅿️

As you leave Rochester, you may notice uncommonly
high numbers of Canada geese. The town is home to
about 30,000, and where they take advantage of the
power-plant warmed-waters of Silver Lake. Light
woods line much of the route to Douglas, and you can
keep track of your progress with the mileage markers.

DOUGLAS (to Pine Island, 8 miles)

Access is in the middle of this very small town
along County Road 14. 🚗 🪵 🅿️ ♿

Check out the Douglas Trading Center Store, including the building out back. Be prepared to meet the

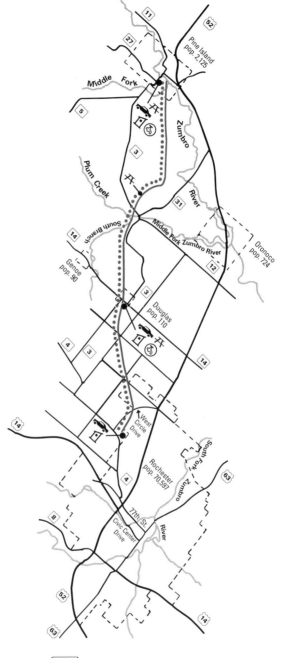

M3 Douglas State Trail

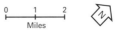

0   1   2
Miles

friendly dog Buddy. Heading north, the trail crosses
the South Branch Middle Fork of the Zumbro River
and, just before Pine Island, the Middle Fork of the
Zumbro River, and in Pine Island, the North Branch
Middle Fork of the Zumbro River.

> **PINE ISLAND**
> Exit Highway 52 at County Road 11 (look for
> signs). Go west on 11 .3 mile. The trail is on
> the south side at Pine Island City Park.
> 🚗 ᴨ 🏠 ♿

More Trail: Citizen groups are forming in the communities of Zumbrota, Mazeppa, and Goodhue for the
purpose of creating the **Goodhue-Pioneer State Trail.**
If successful this trail will connect the Douglas State
Trail to Red Wing.

M4   Duluth Lakewalk
City of Duluth
Primary: One treadway each of asphalt,
boardwalk, crushed rock. 🚶 🚲 ♿
FYI: Horse carriage rides for hire. Crushed
rock treadway for horse carriages only.
Length: 3 miles.
Fees: None.
Recommendation: It's short enough to do it all.
FMI: City of Duluth
　　　　Parks and Recreation
　　　　330 City Hall
　　　　411 West 1st Street
　　　　Duluth, MN 55802
　　　　218-723-3337

　　　　Duluth Area Chamber of Commerce
　　　　118 East Superior Street
　　　　Duluth, MN 55802
　　　　218-722-4011

General Trail Character: In all the exciting lake-front redevelopment, the pedestrian and bicyclist have been
given consideration. Canal Park and the adjacent waterfront development is a collection of business, public, historic, and scenic places in an unsurpassed ocean-
like setting along Lake Superior. Now it's a pedestrian

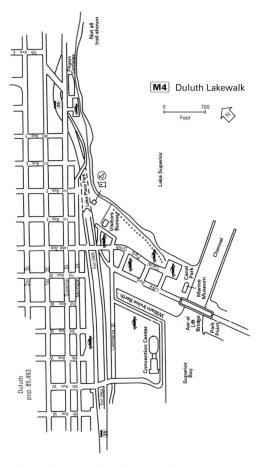

paradise. You can enjoy the water, interpretive signs, maritime artifacts, museums, and the aerial lift bridge and view ships coming and going.

DULUTH

Duluth: Canal Park. Exit I-35 at 5th Avenue West or Lake Avenue. Proceed to lake side of I-35. Most streets take you to the Canal Park area. The Lakewalk is along Lake Superior.

Duluth is the farthest inland seaport in the world, with access via the 2,342-mile Great Lakes–St. Lawrence Seaway system. This Lakewalk is a great way to experience the complexity of a port on a lake. Enjoy the Canal Park Marine Museum, shops and motels, shipping channel viewing plaza, the Fitger

Brewery Complex, and horse carriage rides for hire.
Wander around, on and off the Lakewalk, to really
understand what has been done here. It probably will
be windy.

Something Unique: The whole place is unique for
Minnesota.

More Trail: This section of trail is part of the larger
Waterfront Promenade that may one day connect the
Munger Carlton-West Duluth Trail segment to the
Lakewalk, then north to 60th Street for a distance of
3.5 miles, much of it on railroad right-of-way. Trail is
complete from Canal Park north along the lakeshore,
past Leif Erickson Park, to 26th Avenue East.

M5 Glacial Lakes State Trail

Minnesota Department of Natural Resources,
Trails and Waterways
Primary: Willmar to New London: asphalt.
🚶 🚴 🛼 ♿ 🛷
New London to Hawick: crushed rock.
🚶 🚴 🛷
Hawick to Richmond: original ballast. 🚶 🚴
Secondary: Willmar to New London: natural.
🚶 🐎
FYI: A new trail with substantial development
completed in 1995.
Length: Primary: 36 miles.
       Secondary: 12 miles.
Fees: None.
Recommendation: Willmar to New London.
FMI: DNR Information Center

> Willmar Area Chamber of Commerce
> 518 West Litchfield Avenue
> Willmar, MN 56201
> 612-235-0300

General Trail Character: To recreation planners, central
Minnesota is known as the Central Hills and Lakes
Recreation Landscape. This description is accurate,
and the Glacial Lakes State Trail will immerse you in
it. Expect occasional lakes, wetland complexes, grass-
lands, and lots of fields and farms. The Minnesota

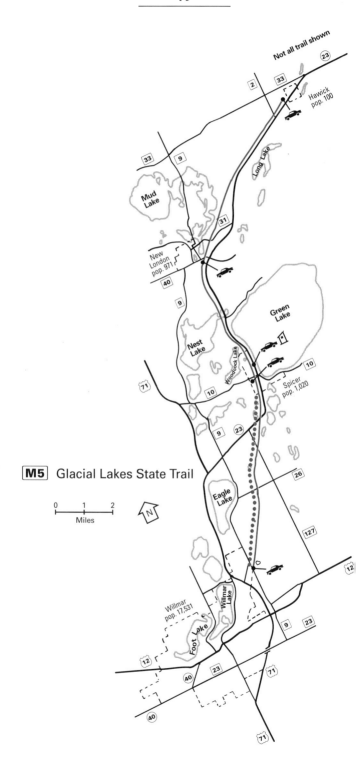

Not all trail shown

Hawick
pop. 100

Long Lake

Mud
Lake

New
London
pop. 971

Green
Lake

Nest
Lake

Woodcock Lake

Spicer
pop. 1,020

M5 Glacial Lakes State Trail

0   1   2
Miles

N

Eagle
Lake

Willmar
Lake

Willmar
pop. 17,531

Foot Lake

State Legislature authorized the Glacial Lakes State
Trail to connect Willmar to St. Cloud, and this portion
is the beginning of the plan. This trail occupies an
abandoned Burlington Northern route that once went
from St. Cloud to Granite Falls and beyond. Portions
are still active.

WILLMAR *(to Spicer, 7 miles)*
Willmar: Northeast of town, within sight of
Civic Center. Along County Road 9 at
intersection with Civic Center Road. 🚗

The glacially shaped landscape is almost immediately
obvious as you leave Willmar, and observe a pattern
of gentle hills and wetland complexes. U. S. Fish and
Wildlife Service Waterfowl Production Areas provide
views of waterfowl and shorebirds. Patches of woods
keep you shaded enough to enjoy the diagonal route
to the Highway 23 underpass and into Spicer.

SPICER *(to New London, 5 miles)*
Spicer: In town at the intersection of Highway
23 and County Road 10. 🚗 🏠 ♿

Here the trail is on the opposite side of the highway
from Green Lake as it passes typical road-side development. Up ahead is a trail bridge over a bay of Nest
Lake, a good spot to stop and linger. New London is a
pretty place of lakes and bays, but you miss most of
the town from the trail. Exit the trail on either County
Road 40 or 31 to get there.

NEW LONDON *(to Hawick, 6 miles)*
New London: South end of town along Highway 23. 🚗

About 3 miles of trail are wooded and peaceful and
some distance from Highway 23. At the Long Lake
area the landscape opens up considerably, Highway 23
ventures very close, and it's a straight, open shot into
Hawick.

HAWICK *(to Richmond, 18 miles)*
Hawick: Along Highway 23. Road parking. 🚗

No development is currently planned for this long section to Richmond.

M6 Heartland State Trail

Minnesota Department of Natural Resources, Trails and Waterways
Primary: Park Rapids to Walker: asphalt.
🚶 🚴 ♿ 🛷
Walker to Cass Lake: original ballast.
🚶 🚴 🛷 🐎
Secondary: Natural. 🚶 🛷 🚴 🐎
FYI: The Park Rapids to Walker segment is an older asphalt trail only 6 feet wide. Parts of it are quite rough. Rehabilitation is planned for 1996.
Length: 48 miles.
Fees: Great Minnesota Ski Pass.
Recommendation: Park Rapids to Nevis and Akeley to Walker. Don't miss Lake Belle Taine.
FMI: DNR Information Center

> Park Rapids Area Chamber of Commerce
> Highway 71 South
> Park Rapids, MN 56470
> 218-732-4111
> 800-247-0054

General Trail Character: Expect a warm welcome from the little towns in this major resort area. This line was built by the Park Rapids and Leech Lake Railway Company and completed in 1898. In 1907 it was sold to the Great Northern Railway, who operated it for 63 years. Timber and agricultural products were moved in enormous quantities, and the last passenger train ran in 1952. The Great Northern merged into the Burlington Northern in 1970, and the line was abandoned in 1972. The trail passes through a transition area of farms to Minnesota's wooded north country.

> **PARK RAPIDS** *(to Dorset, 6 miles; to Nevis, 6 miles)*
> **Park Rapids:** Heartland County Park. Exit State Highway 34 at Mill Road (opposite Harbor Restaurant). Go north to park. 🚻 🪧 🏕 ♿
> **Dorset:** Downtown, along State Highway 226. 🚻 🪧 🏕 ♿

The farms, woods, and prairie environment start right away when you leave Park Rapids and continue to Dorset. You pass a fire tower along the way. Some

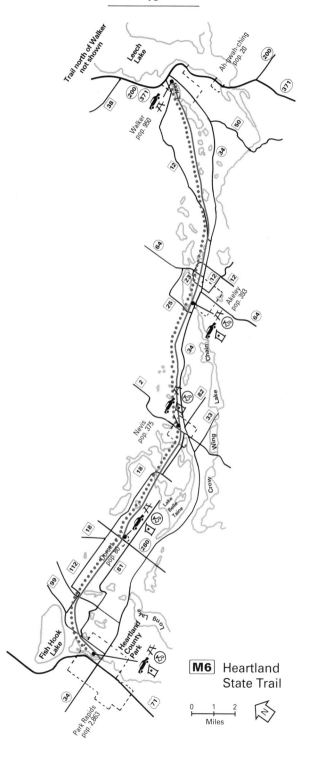

Trail north of Walker
not shown

Leech Lake

Ah-gwah-ching
pop. 20

200

371

38 200 371

Walker
pop. 950

50

34

12

64

12

23 112 12

25 Aveley
pop. 383

64

34 Chain

2 82 Lake

Nevis
pop. 375

33

Wing

18 Crow

Lake
Belle
Taine

18 Dorset
pop. 60

112 280

99 81

Long Lake

Fish Hook
Lake

Heartland
County Park

34 71

Park Rapids
pop. 2,863

M6 Heartland
State Trail

0   1   2
Miles

N

cities along trails seem to have fun, and Dorset (pop. 50?) is one of them. It advertises itself as the city "that prides itself in selling off the mayor's office in a raffle." You can also get Mexican food here. Stop at Lake Belle Taine to enjoy the views. There are other lakes, but this is one of the best.

NEVIS (Akeley, 6 miles; to Walker, 10 miles)
Nevis: Downtown, along County Road 2.
🚗 🏕 🍴 ♿
Akeley: West side of downtown. Look for signs on Highway 34. 🚗 🏕 🍴 ♿

Nevis is next, complete with the world's largest tiger-muskie statue, located in a public park along the trail. A bakery and coffeeshop are nearby too. The stretch to Akeley is close to Highway 34, and by now you are really sensing that the transition to woods is over. By the time you get past Akeley, the trail is intimately boxed in by tall trees. Still more lakes appear before you reach Walker and the end of the developed right-of-way. There are mileage markers along the way.

WALKER (to Cass Lake, 21 miles)
Walker: Lake May, west side of town. Exit State Highway 371 (look for signs) south on county Road 12, go .5 mile. 🚗 🏕

The trail north of Walker offers views of Leech Lake, one of Minnesota's largest, and closely parallels Hwy. 371 for most of the way. No new development is planned at this time.

CASS LAKE
Cass Lake: Trail ends 2 miles south of town along Highway 371. Road parking. 🚗

Something Unique: Lake Belle Taine epitomizes a north-woods lake.

More Trail: The Heartland and **Paul Bunyan State Trail** will be one and the same from about 4 miles west of Walker to two miles north, when development of the Paul Bunyan is complete.

M7 Hennepin Parks Southwest Regional Light Rail Transit Trail – Northern Route

Hennepin Parks

Primary: Crushed rock. 𝑀 𖾻 𝑍 𝒸 𝑀 (some snowmobiling is allowed from Victoria to Shorewood and skiing elsewhere but parts of the trail are plowed for winter pedestrian use.)

FYI: Some bridges are missing. Detours are provided.

Length: 15.7 miles.

Fees: None.

Recommendation: For a wilder experience try Victoria to Excelsior. If the action and activity of attractive cities interests you try, Hopkins / Minnetonka.

FMI: Hennepin Parks
French Regional Park
12615 County Road 9
Plymouth, MN 55441-1248
612-559-9000

Twin West Chamber of Commerce
10550 Wayzata Boulevard
Minnetonka, MN
612-540-0234

General Trail Character: Hennepin Parks Light Rail Transit (LRT) trails are new, significant, and even dramatic, especially this northern route. This trail and the next are the property of the Hennepin County Regional Railroad Authority and are designated as future light-rail transit corridors. Recreation is allowed as an interim use and is managed by Hennepin Parks. Most recently this scenic trail was part of the Chicago and North Western Transportation system before being purchased by Hennepin County Regional Railroad Authority. The trail travels the lake-dotted landscape of the western suburbs.

HOPKINS (to Minnetonka (I-494), 2.9 miles; to Deephaven, 3.9 miles, to Excelsior, 2.4 miles)

Hopkins: Use Park and Ride lot at County Road 3 and 8th Avenue South. Go north on 8th three blocks to 1st Street North to find trail. 🚗

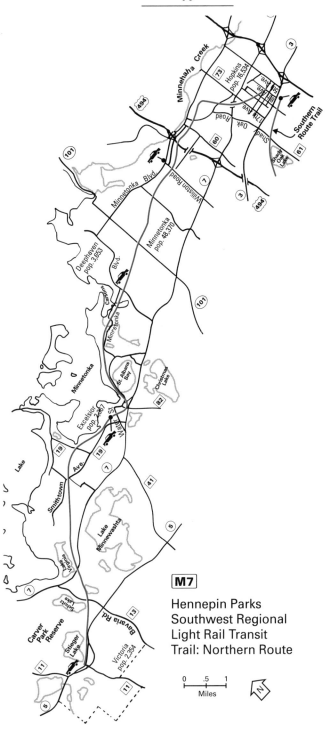

M7

Hennepin Parks
Southwest Regional
Light Rail Transit
Trail: Northern Route

0   .5   1
Miles

N

Minnetonka: Civic Center on north side of Highway 5 at Williston Road. Trail is on south side of Highway. 🚗

Deephaven: Minnetonka Boulevard at Carson's Bay. Use Park and Ride facility. 🚗

This trail, together with the Southern Route trail, makes Hopkins a trail hub. The two trail ends are only 3 blocks apart. From the Hopkins access you will get a good look at downtown, front and back. The attractive and well-designed trail takes you next to Minnetonka, which has its own extensive system of trails. In Minnetonka you will skim past parks and trail intersections that deserve exploration if you have time. The route to Deephaven is a series of cuts and fills through the landscape and offers a long view of Carson's Bay. Expect occasional glimpses of beautiful Lake Minnetonka as you skirt the shoreline to St. Albans Bay. At the Bay the railroad bridge is gone, but there are plans to replace it soon. Use Minnetonka Boulevard in the interim.

EXCELSIOR (to Victoria, 6.5 miles)

Excelsior: West edge of downtown by Excelsior Mill shopping area. Parking in vicinity. 🚗

Visiting Excelsior is fun as the trail brings you to the edge of a well-developed downtown. The way to Victoria has a landscape of more hills and lakes, nice homes, and interesting railroad cuts and fills. Victoria, along with the huge Carver Park Reserve, is at the southwest corner of Lake Minnetonka. There are accesses from the trail into Carver Park, but even if you don't enter, you get plenty of long views of wooded hills, lakes, and wetlands.

VICTORIA

Victoria: .4 mile west of State Highway 5 along Steiger Lake Lane. Across street from Victoria House. 🚗

Something Unique: Lake Minnetonka has been described as Minnesota's most beautiful lake and the views from the trail are excellent.

More Trail: A proposed north-south trail from Victoria to Chaska which would create a triangle of trails. At Hopkins it's only a short distance to the **Southern Route LRT Trail.**

M8 Hennepin Parks Southwest Regional Light Rail Transit Trail – Southern Route

Includes **City of Chanhassen Trail** (M8-A)
Hennepin Parks
Primary: Crushed rock. 🚶 🚴 🏇 ♿ 🛷 (some snowmobiling is allowed at the southwest end)
FYI: Some bridges are missing. Detours are provided.
Length: 11.5 miles.
Fees: None.
Recommendation: Try Miller's Park to Bluff Creek Road or vice versa. This has some curves and elevated views.
FMI: Hennepin Parks
　　　 French Lake Regional Park
　　　 12615 County Road 9
　　　 Plymouth, MN 55441-1248
　　　 612-559-9000

　　　 Twin West Chamber of Commerce
　　　 10550 Wayzata Boulevard
　　　 Minnetonka, MN
　　　 612-540-0234

General Trail Character: This southern route is the shorter and younger (by one year) cousin to the northern route. It too occupies a former Chicago and North Western corridor and consists of 10.7 miles of Hennepin County Regional Railroad Authority property and about .8 mile of City of Chanhassen right-of-way.

HOPKINS (to Eden Prairie, 6 miles)
Hopkins: Intersection of Highway 3 and 8th Avenue South at the Park and Ride parking lot. Look for small signs on Highway 3. 🚗

Although there is more HCRRA right-of-way to the east, the trail begins at Highway 3 and 8th Avenue South. As you leave downtown Hopkins, you will soon pass Shady Oak Lake, with the trail hugging the north shore for about a .5 mile. Expect then to see scattered development with some woods and wetlands in between.

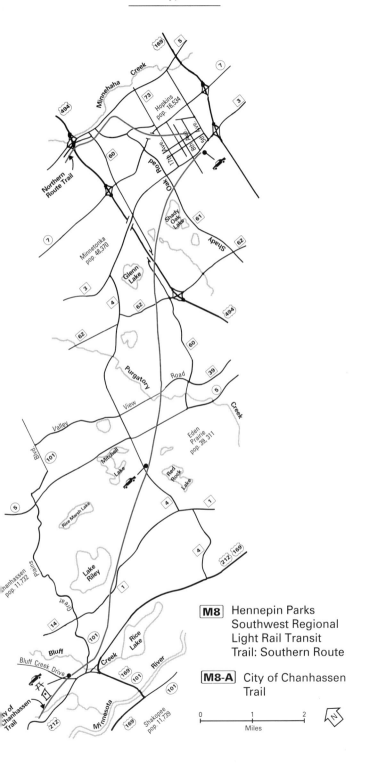

M8 Hennepin Parks
Southwest Regional
Light Rail Transit
Trail: Southern Route

M8-A City of Chanhassen
Trail

0   1   2
Miles

EDEN PRAIRIE (to Chanhassen, 5.5 miles)
Eden Prairie: Miller Park on Eden Prairie
Road (County Road 4), just north of trail. 🚗

Much of the trail is a repeating series of cuts and fills,
especially from Eden Prairie south. Before long you
pass by Riley Lake, a significant scenic spot. The very
southwestern end of the trail is tucked halfway up the
side of the Minnesota River valley bluffs, and you
have views across the valley to Shakopee.

CHANHASSEN
Chanhassen: At Bluff Creek Drive, just uphill
form U. S. Highway 212. 🚗 🏕 🚻

More Trail: In Hopkins, follow 8th Avenue South to
get to the **Northern Route LRT Trail.**

M9 Luce Line State Trail
Includes City of Plymouth Trail (M9-A), City
of Hutchinson Trail (M9-B)
Minnesota Department of Natural Resources,
Trails and Waterways
Primary:
Plymouth (I-494) to Vicksburg Lane: asphalt.
🚶 🚲 🚃 ♿
Vicksburg Lane to Orono (Stubbs Bay Road):
crushed rock. 🚶 🚲 ⛷ ♿
Stubbs Bay Road to Winsted: crushed rock.
🚶 🚲 ♿ ❄
Winsted to Hutchinson: natural. 🚶 🚵 ❄ 🐎
Hutchinson: crushed rock. 🚶 🚲 ♿
Hutchinson to Cosmos: natural. 🚶 🚵 ❄ 🐎
(caution—bridges out)
Cosmos to Lake Thompson: crushed rock.
🚶 🚲 ❄ 🐎
Secondary: Plymouth (Vicksburg Lane) to
Winsted: natural. 🚶 ⛷ 🐎
FYI: The easterly 1.1 miles of trail is owned
and maintained by the City of Plymouth.
Hutchinson has nearly finished connecting the
Luce Line to fill that 1.9-mile gap. The DNR
plans some rehabilitation of existing surfaces,
perhaps in 1996.
Length: 64 miles.

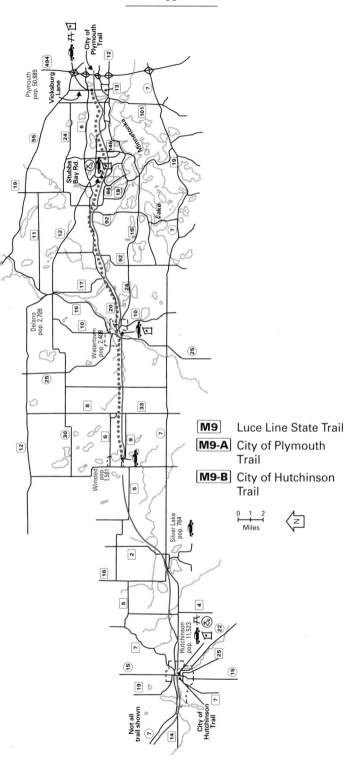

M9 Luce Line State Trail

M9-A City of Plymouth Trail

M9-B City of Hutchinson Trail

Fees: Great Minnesota Ski Pass.
Recommendation: With long trails it's hard to recommend just one stretch. But try Vicksburg Lane Access west, Winsted going east, or the Watertown vicinity.
FMI: DNR Information Center

> Hutchinson Area Convention and
> Visitors Bureau
> 45 Washington Avenue East
> Hutchinson, MN 55350
> 612-587-5252

> Twin West Chamber of Commerce
> 10550 Wayzata Boulevard
> Minnetonka, MN 55343
> 612-540-0234

General Trail Character: The Luce Line is one of Minnesota's oldest rail-trails, having been purchased in 1974–1975, and it offers a quiet experience so close to the Twin Cities. Railroad plans were often bigger than the reality that developed, as was the case here. Mr. W. L. Luce tried to develop the Luce Electric Short Line Railway from Minneapolis to Brookings, but he only made it to Gluck, in 1927. Eventually the line ended up as part of the Chicago North Western Transportation Company system and was abandoned in 1971. Trail development is uneven but advancing in fits and starts, with the more developed lengths at the Twin Cities end (except for two miles in Hutchinson).

PLYMOUTH (to Orono [Stubbs Bay], 6 miles; to Watertown, 12 miles)

Plymouth: On Vicksburg Lane, .5 mile south of County Road 6.
Orono: Stubbs Bay Road, one mile south of State Highway 12.

Lakes are numerous in the western suburbs of the Twin Cities, and you don't go far on the Luce Line before crossing a bay of Gleason Lake. Views of woods, wetlands, and development dominate. Slowly but surely the transition from suburban to rural happens, and the landscape opens up some from the well-wooded beginnings. There are numerous well-marked road crossings. Just before Watertown is Oak Lake, and the trail causeway puts water on both sides.

WATERTOWN *(to Winsted, 10 miles; to Silver Lake, 8 miles; to Hutchinson, 7 miles)*

Watertown: Downtown. From intersection of Carver County 20 and Lewis Avenue Southwest, go south on Lewis two blocks to Madison, then east 1 block to trail. 🚗 🏠

Winsted: Southeast part of town at County Road 9 and 235th Street. Well marked once you get there. There is no access to the west. 🚗

Silver Lake: Trail bisects this small town. Street parking. 🚗

Watertown is on the banks of the South Fork Crow River and the downtown Veterans' Memorial Park offers water. Enjoy the Midwestern main street from one of the park benches. After Watertown is a fairly straight shot to Winsted. Just before you enter town is a nice piece of trail along Winsted Lake. There is a one mile gap in the trail at Winsted and city streets provide a bypass. The quality of the surface deteriorates by Silver Lake where you encounter a two-block length of muddy trail. A parallel city street is slightly better to use.

HUTCHINSON *(to Cosmos, 17 miles)*

Hutchinson: Old Fellows or Masonic / West River Park. From State Highway 7/22 go south on School Road one block. Parks are along the water's edge. 🚗 🏕 🏠 ♿

At Hutchinson the city has done wonders to thread the trail through town past Otter Lake, the Crow River, connecting several waterfront parks. A gap still persists on the east side of town. The surface from Hutchinson toward Cosmos has recently been graded, smoothed, and seeded. East of Cosmos the trail parallels Highway 7 through a agricultural landscape with an occasional wetland and wooded area. Some bridges are missing.

COSMOS

Cosmos: Cosmos County Park, one mile west of town on State Highway 7. 🚗 🏕 🏠 ♿

Cosmos County Park on Lake Thompson is attractive, and the trail starts right there. Unfortunately only the short length to Cosmos is developed, and to get through town you must use Highway 7.

More Trail: This trail will be extended 6 miles eastward to Theodore Wirth Park by Hennepin Parks and will be a rails-with-trails project on a Chicago and North Western line.

M10 Minnesota Valley Trail State Park

Minnesota Department of Natural Resources,
Parks and Recreation
Primary: Asphalt. 🚶 🚴 🛷 ♿ ⛷
Length: 5 miles.
Fees: Great Minnesota Ski Pass.
Recommendation: You must visit the swing
bridge and the shortest way is to start at the
Chaska access.
FMI: DNR Information Center

> Shakopee Area Chamber of Commerce
> 1801 East Highway 101
> Shakopee, MN 55379
> 612-445-1660

General Trail Character: The Minnesota Valley Trail
State Park offers remarkable recreation opportunities,
considering its close proximity to the Twin Cites. This
5 miles of rail-trail is well-developed and is the middle
portion of a planned 75-mile system. This line originally started out as the Hastings and Dakota Railway,
a division of the Chicago, Milwaukee and St. Paul
Railroad, and it connected the end points described in
its name by 1879. The Minnesota Valley Trail State
Park has one of the longest trestles on any trail in
Minnesota, the Chaska Swing Bridge. Built in 1900
and weighing 300 tons, it could be opened by one per-
son turning a crank.

SHAKOPEE (to Highway 41, 4.3 miles; to Chaska, .7 miles)

Shakopee: Veterans' Memorial Park, east side
of town along State Highway 101. 🚗 🅿 🍽 ♿
Highway 41: Signed between Chaska and U.S.
Highway 169. A dirt trail connects this access
to the rail-trail. 🚗 🅿

This trail has steadily advanced through Shakopee
and now runs the entire length of town between Highway 101 and the Minnesota River. For a short while
things do get noisy near the highway, but the calm
soon returns. On the way to Chaska expect to be surprised at the wildness you go through. Take time to
read the interpretive signs about the Shakopee Brewery, where a spring, the northern cool exposure, and

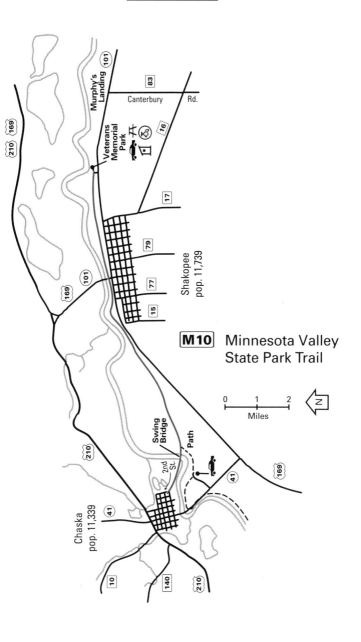

M10 Minnesota Valley
State Park Trail

access to ice created a choice spot for Herman Strunk's
endeavor. Between the Highway 41 access and Chaska
is the Swing Bridge. Steps at each end allow you to go
below for a better view. The short stretch of trail left to
Chaska received some damage from the 1993 floods,
and temporary repairs have been made.

CHASKA

Chaska: Next to Courthouse Complex. Exit
State Highway 41 on 2nd Street and follow to
trail. 🚗

Something Unique: The Minnesota DNR, Division of
Parks and Recreation, Interpretive Services, has a
great little brochure about the Swing Bridge.

More Trail: At the Highway 41 access is more natural-
surface trail to the south.

M11 Paul Bunyan State Trail

Minnesota Department of Natural Resources,
Trails and Waterways
Primary:
Brainerd to Hackensack: asphalt.
🚶 🚲 🛷 ♿ 🛶
Hackensack to Bemidji: original ballast.
🚶 🚵 🛶
Lake Bemidji State Park Vicinity: asphalt.
🚶 🚲 🛷 ♿ 🛶
FYI: No improvements from Walker to near
Bemidji are budgeted now. The right-of-way is
not continuous in and near Walker.
Length: 100 miles.
Fees: Great Minnesota Ski Pass.
Recommendation: Brainerd to Nisswa. Don't
miss Lake Hubert as a rest stop.
FMI: DNR Information Center

Brainerd Lakes Area Chamber of
Commerce
6th & Washington
Brainerd, MN 56401
218-829-2838

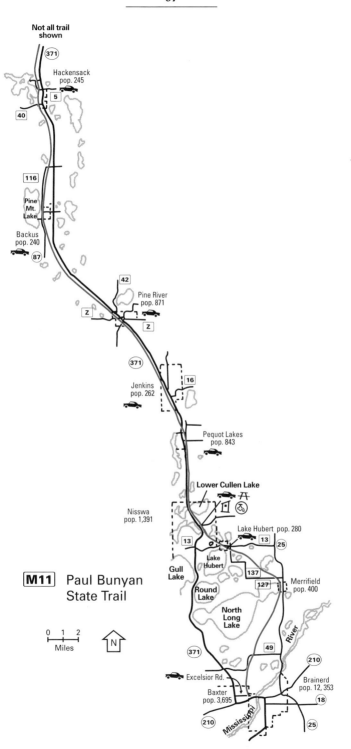

Not all trail shown

371

Hackensack
pop. 245

5

40

116

Pine Mt. Lake

Backus
pop. 240

87

42

Pine River
pop. 871

Z

Z

371

Jenkins
pop. 262

16

Pequot Lakes
pop. 843

Lower Cullen Lake

Nisswa
pop. 1,391

Lake Hubert pop. 280

13

1

13

25

M11 Paul Bunyan
State Trail

Gull
Lake

Lake
Hubert

137

Merrifield
pop. 400

127

0 1 2
Miles

N

Round
Lake

North
Long
Lake

River

371

49

210

Excelsior Rd.

Brainerd
pop. 12, 353

210

18

Baxter
pop. 3,695

210

Mississippi

25

General Trail Character: The Paul Bunyan State Trail is another new and long rail-trail for Minnesota, traveling near dozens of scenic lakes. The trail was made possible by the abandonment of a lengthy Burlington Northern right-of-way. For most of this line's existence it was operated by the Northern Pacific Railway and hauled the logs from the extensive pine forests of north-central Minnesota. A 1950's caboose is on display along the trail in downtown Nisswa. From the Paul Bunyan you will see lots of woods, especially at the southern end and the northern one-third.

BRAINERD (to Lake Hubert, 13 miles; to Nisswa, 2 miles)

Brainerd: West side. From U. S. Highway 371 just north of U. S. Highway 210 exit east onto Excelsior Road. Trail is in about .6 mile. 🚗

The first 10 miles of this wooded trail make a big loop around North Long Lake. At Merrifield you get your first good views of the big lake followed by Lake Hubert. Don't miss visiting the 1896 Lake Hubert Depot, billed as the only open-air railway station remaining in the country.

NISSWA (to Pequot Lakes, 6 miles; to Jenkins, 3 miles; to Pine River, 6 miles; to Hackensack, 16 miles; to Walker, 17 miles)

Nisswa: Downtown; by caboose. 🚗 ⛱ ⑴ ♿
Pequot Lakes, Jenkins, Pine River, Backus, Hackensack: Trail can easily be found along Highway 371. 🚗

It is a short trip from Lake Hubert to Nisswa, another pleasant place to stop. On the haul toward Walker, you will not be far from Highway 371. The right-of-way is less wooded than the surrounding landscape. In the open areas are prairie grasses such as big bluestem. Travel north of Hackensack will be on the loose, sandy, original ballast.

About five miles south of Walker, there is a gap in DNR ownership of the right-of-way. Plans are to take the trail cross-country to the west and link with the Heartland State Trail. Snowmobile use of this route is now possible. For other uses, you will have to end your trip south of town or brave Highway 371 to continue to Walker.

WALKER (to Benedict, 8 miles; to LaPorte, 5 miles;
to Guthrie, 6 miles; to Nary, 6 miles; to Beltrami /
Hubbard County Line, 3.5 miles
Walker: Use Heartland State Trail Access.
Exit Highway 371 (look for signs) south on
County Road 12, go .5 mile.
Benedict, LaPorte, Guthrie, Nary: Trail goes
through or next to these very small towns.
Street parking.

It's a long stretch to the finish in Bemidji, past very
small towns, lakes, wetlands, fields, tamarack bogs,
and more woods. When completed, the Paul Bunyan
State Trail will be a long and wild ride.

BEMIDJI
Bemidji: South of town. From U. S. Highway
71 exit east on County Road 35, go .75 mile to
trail on south side. Road parking.

DNR right-of-way ownership begins / ends at this
Beltrami / Hubbard County line.

BEMIDJI STATE PARK UNITS
North Unit. Northeast side of Lake
Bemidji.

There is a 4-mile length of paved trail from the park's
south unit on the east side of Lake Bemidji (near
County Road 12) to the north unit.

Something Unique: Lake Hubert with the open-air
station and the Lake Hubert Store.

More Trail: Acquisition of additional right-of-way into
Bemidji is being contemplated. Ultimately the Paul
Bunyan is to end at the north unit of Lake Bemidji
State Park, creating a connection to the **Blue Ox Trail.**

M12 Richard J. Dorer Memorial Hardwood State Forest–Hay Creek Management Unit Trail

Minnesota Department of Natural Resources, Forestry

Primary: Natural. 🏃 ⛷ 🐎

FYI: For the most part undeveloped. Be prepared.

Length: 8.9 miles.

Fees: Great Minnesota Ski Pass.

Recommendation: Best to start out from the trail access in the Hay Creek unit. Either direction is good.

FMI: Minnesota DNR Information Center

> Red Wing Area Chamber of Commerce
> 420 Levee Street
> Red Wing, MN 55066
> 612-388-4719
> 800-762-9516

General Trail Character: This right-of-way was acquired by the State of Minnesota as part of the Richard J. Dorer Memorial Hardwood State Forest in 1970. Since then very little development has occurred, and it remains substantially a wild place. State-forest land ownership in the valley totals about 1500 acres, and it is managed for recreation, wildlife, and forest products. This route was part of the Chicago Great Western system, which connected Red Wing to Rochester. In 1968 the CGW merged with the Chicago and North Western railroad. This company has dismantled much of this system in the Midwest, creating numerous rail-trail opportunities.

HAY CREEK MANAGEMENT UNIT

Red Wing: From Highway 61 and County Boulevard 1 junction in Red Wing go 2 miles south on County Boulevard 1, then left on Pioneer Road about .3 mile to access on right. Street parking. 🚗

Hay Creek Management Unit: From Highway 61/58 junction in Red Wing go 6 miles south to Hay Creek Trail (a road), which is at the very little town of Hay

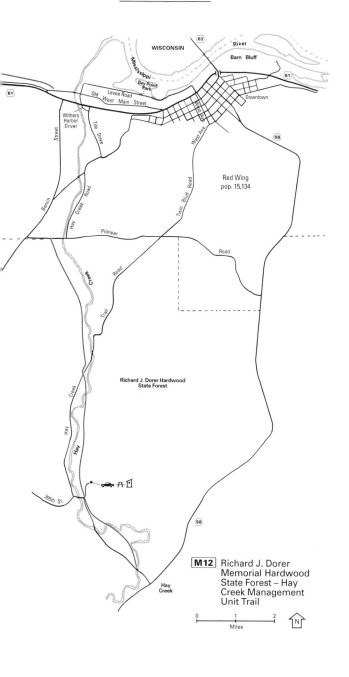

WISCONSIN

River

Barn Bluff

63

61

Mississippi

Bay Point Park

Levee Road

Old West Main Street

Downtown

61

Withers Harbor Driver

Street

Tile Drive

West Ave.

58

Bench

Hay Creek Road

Twin Bluff Road

Red Wing
pop. 15,134

Pioneer

Road

Creek

Road

Trail

Richard J. Dorer Hardwood
State Forest

Creek

Hay

Hay

305th St.

58

Hay
Creek

M12 Richard J. Dorer
Memorial Hardwood
State Forest – Hay
Creek Management
Unit Trail

0   1   2
Miles

N

Creek. Turn right, and you will see the trail on the right in .25 mile. Go one mile to a developed-trail access. ⊸ ⼝ ⊡

This is a minimally maintained trail in a wild valley. Expect occasional muddy conditions. The trail is heavily wooded and exceptionally scenic. Lands along both sections are hunted in the fall. Turkey hunting in the spring is common. Occupying the valley center is Hay Creek, a popular and productive cold-water trout stream.

More Trail: Due to corridor conditions, use of the 5 miles of right-of-way south of Hay Creek Trail (a road) is not recommended.

M13 Root River State Trail

Includes **Harmony-Preston Valley State Trail** (M13-A)
Minnesota Department of Natural Resources, Trails and Waterways
Primary: Asphalt. 🏃 🚴 🛷 ⛷ ♿
FYI: The western end is steep for a rail-trail (4%). Coasting for 5 miles is possible (but it's work when going up). Many choose to start somewhere in the middle, head west (uphill) and then enjoy the ride back.
Length: 35.3 miles.
Fees: Great Minnesota Ski Pass.
Recommendation: Start at Lanesboro. Go west to Isinours. Then decide if you want to go up the hill or not. Going east to Whalan is pleasant and less strenuous.
FMI: DNR Information Center

> Root River Trail Towns
> Box 398
> Lanesboro, MN 55949
>
> Lanesboro Tourist Information
> P. O. Box 20,
> Lanesboro, MN 55949
> 800-944-2670

General Trail Character: This trail is one of the best. What makes it so is the dramatic landscape of southeast Minnesota and the character of the small river

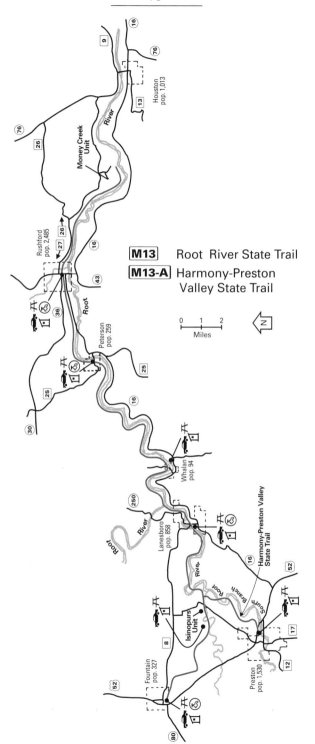

M13 Root River State Trail

M13-A Harmony-Preston Valley State Trail

0 1 2
Miles

N

towns along the way. The Root River State Trail parallels the Root River for nearly 30 miles, and when not
near the river the trail crosses beautiful tributaries with
48 bridges. This railroad line got started in 1865 as the
Southern Minnesota Railroad Company and was part
of the 162-mile line from the Mississippi River to
Winnebago, Minnesota. Hauling wheat, lumber, and
people, it went bankrupt in 1871 and was purchased
by the Chicago, Milwaukee and St. Paul Railway in
1880. They operated it as part of the Milwaukee Road
until it was abandoned in 1979. Make this a two-day
trip so you have plenty of time to linger and wander.

FOUNTAIN (to Lanesboro, 11.2 miles)
Fountain: East side of town on County Road
8. Look for signs. ⇝ ⅋ 🏠 ♿

If you start at Fountain, in about .5 mile you pass a
sinkhole, then descend into a wooded valley, criss-
crossing Watson Creek along the way. The scenery of
southeastern Minnesota gets better and better. The
Isinours unit of the Richard J. Dorer Memorial Hardwood Forest at about mile 5.5, is a nice rest stop (all
that coasting is work!). You will then cross the South
Branch Root River three times before Lanesboro. This
section also includes a short but dramatic rock cut by
the Old Barn Resort.

LANESBORO (to Whalan, 4.6 miles; to Peterson, 8.9 miles)
Lanesboro: Downtown. Trail Center is below
Museum, right on trail (scheduled to be moved
to a new replica depot one block further east
in 1996). ⇝ ⅋ 🏠 ♿
Whalan: Downtown. ⇝ ⅋

Lanesboro is made for trail users. Built around water
power and milling, the entire downtown is a National
Historic District. You will want to explore places like
the Das Wurst Haus. To say more might spoil it. Now
down in the valley, you'll find the smaller towns of
Whalan and Peterson. They have character and enjoy
trail visitors. Make time for the rest areas and ice-
cream shops. Along the way keep a lookout for wild
turkeys and rattlesnakes as the wooded slopes and
rock outcrops are a great habitat. Neither will bother
you if left alone.

PETERSON (to Rushford, 4.8 miles, to Money Creek Woods, 5.8 miles)

Peterson: Along bluff edge of downtown.
🚐 ⛽ 🏠 ⛲

Rushford: Signs on State Highway 16.
One block north of 16, then west side of road at South Elm Street. 🚐 ⛽ 🏠 ⛲

From Peterson to Rushford the valley opens up, and the trail and Highway 16 travel together to Rushford. The Rushford Depot Museum serves as another nice rest stop. There is a two-block gap in the trail if you go farther east. The last 5.8 miles to Money Creek Woods forest unit extends the same great trail qualities but dead-ends there.

Something Unique: Near mile 7, at the bridge over the South Branch Root River, is a "telltale." Go find out what that is!

More Trail: The Blufflands Trail System is a state-legislature approved concept for a 120-mile system of trails connecting many communities of southeastern Minnesota. The **Harmony–Preston Valley State Trail** will be a 17-mile trail from the Root River State Trail at the Isinours Unit to Preston and Harmony. The 5.5 miles from Isinours to Preston opened late 1995 and adds more terrific scenery. Land acquisition has begun for a 5-mile extension from Money Creek Woods to Houston.

M14 Sakatah Singing Hills State Trail

Minnesota Department of Natural Resources, Trails and Waterways
Primary: Asphalt. 🚶 🚴 🛷 ⛷ 🛶
Length: 39 miles.
Fees: Great Minnesota Ski Pass.
Recommendation: The Mankato end and Sakatah Lake State Park are both great places to visit.
FMI: Minnesota DNR Information Center

Mankato Area Chamber of Commerce
P. O. Box 999
Mankato, MN 56002
507-345-4519

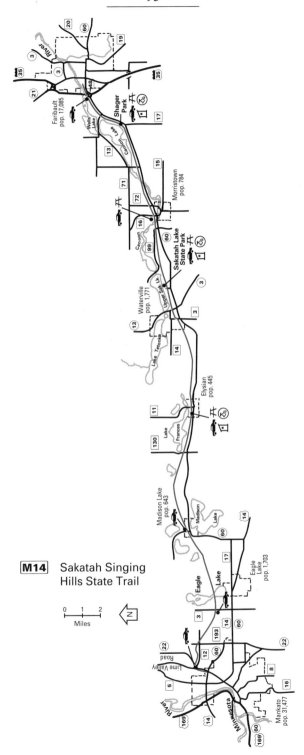

M14 Sakatah Singing Hills State Trail

Faribault Area Chamber of Commerce
530 Wilson Avenue North West
Faribault, MN 55021
507-334-4381

General Trail Character: The Sakatah Singing Hills State
Trail travels through a glaciated landscape of lakes,
rivers, and gently rolling countryside now occupied by
farms, resorts, small towns, wildlife areas, parks, and a
touch of surburbia on the east end. It is a popular
snowmobile route. The right-of-way, originally built in
1882 by the Minnesota Central Railroad, connected
Red Wing and Mankato. The eastern 20 miles of this
route is now the Cannon Valley Trail. The line was
purchased for trail purposes in 1971. Native Americans
called this area Sakatah, the Dakota word for singing
hills. This lightly wooded trail in an agricultural landscape occasionally passes lakes and wetlands. Over
half of the trail closely parallels Highway 60.

> ### MANKATO (to Eagle Lake, 5 miles; to Madison Lake,
> ### 5 miles; to Elysian, 7 miles; to Waterville, 6 miles)
> **Mankato:** Take State Highway 22.5 miles
> north of State Highway 60 to Lime Valley
> Road, then turn left to trail access. 🚗
> **Eagle Lake:** Take County Road 3 one mile
> north of Highway 60 to trail parking area. 🚗
> **Madison Lake:** From Highway 60 take Main
> Street north to trail. 🚗
> **Elysian:** Along Highway 60 on west side of
> town at LeSueur County Museum. 🚗 🏕 🏛
> ♿

From the access at Mankato the first 2 miles (there are
markers) wind up a heavily wooded valley inhabited
by an attractive creek. A trail bridge over the water puts
you about 50 feet in the air, and it is not for the faint of
heart. After these 2 miles you are on top of the landscape and ready to head out into the open route to
Faribault. Below the Mankato access is another .5
mile of trail, which connects to the Mankato city trail
system.

> ### WATERVILLE (to Sakatah Lake State Park, 2 miles;
> ### to Morristown, 4 miles; to Shager Park, 5 miles;
> ### to Faribault, 4 miles)
> **Waterville:** Sakatah Lake State Park 2 miles
> east of town along Highway 60 (park sticker

required for vehicles). 🚲 ⍭ 🏠 ♿
Morristown: Along north side of Highway
60. 🚲 ⍭
Shager Park: Well marked from Highway 60,
4 miles west of Faribault. 🚲 ⍭ 🏠 ♿

A .5 mile gap exists in Waterville and marked city streets provide the link. Sakatah Lake State Park is a mostly wooded, pleasant place with 3.5 miles of shore along Upper Sakatah Lake. The trail travels the whole length of the park, and the amenities make for a enjoyable rest stop. Shager Park offers public access to Cannon Lake.

FARIBAULT
Faribault: On north side of Highway 60, two blocks west of I-35. Also look for access signs along Highway 21. 🚲

More Trail: In Faribault there is 1 mile of trail farther into town, ending 3 blocks east of King Mill Park.

M15 Stone Arch Bridge
Minneapolis Park and Recreation Board
Primary: Asphalt. 🏃 🚲 🛼 ♿
Length: .4 mile.
Fees: None.
Recommendation: Be sure to visit the west-bank end.
FMI: Minneapolis Park and Recreation Board
200 Grain Exchange
400 South 4th Street
Minneapolis, MN 55415
612-661-4800

General Trail Character: The Minneapolis riverfront, near downtown and occupying both banks of the Mississippi River, is undergoing rapid redevelopment that promises to put people, parks and beauty back along the water's edge. In the center of this complex mix is the stunning Stone Arch Bridge gracefully stepping across the river in a curved 2,100-foot long route. This 23-arch bridge was built by the Minneapolis Union Railway Company and James J. Hill in 1882 to 1883. In its 1948 heyday, 82 passenger trains a day used the

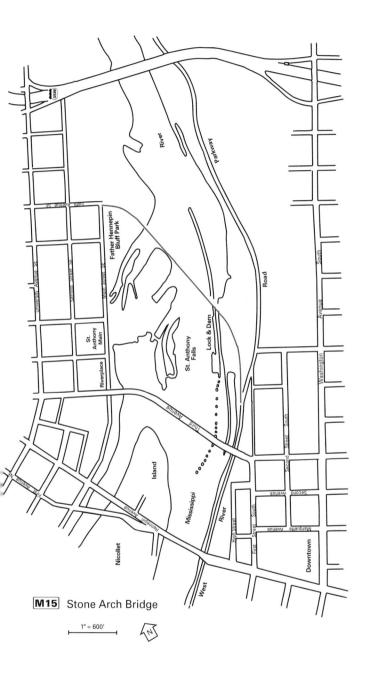

M15 Stone Arch Bridge

1" = 600'

bridge to the downtown depots. The last passenger train was in 1978, and restoration was recently completed. It is now owned by the Minnesota Department of Transportation.

MINNEAPOLIS (East and West Banks of the Mississippi River)
East Bank: Street or pay-lot parking. 🚗
West Bank: Street or pay-lot parking. 🚗

At this National Historic Engineering Landmark, there are long views up and down the river. Interpretive signs at the west bank offer details about the bridge's construction, use, and redevelopment. Watch the activities at the lock and dam and explore the other elements of the Minneapolis riverfront.

More Trail: Connects to the **West River Parkway** and will ultimately connect to the **Cedar Lake Trail.**

M16–17–18, 18-A
Willard Munger State Trail

The Minnesota Department of Natural Resources, with legislative and citizen support, has in mind a recreational trail from St. Paul to Duluth, Minnesota's two largest metropolitan areas. A substantial amount of this is done, making extensive use of railroad rights-of-way. The Gateway segment connects St. Paul to near Stillwater, and Hinckley to Duluth is only interrupted by a 3 mile road route south of Carlton. These trails, and their segments, are described on the following pages.

Not often is a trail named for a current state legislator, but Representative Willard Munger of Duluth is a tremendous advocate of outdoor recreation and natural resource stewardship. He has served since 1955 and currently sits on the Legislative Commission on Minnesota Resources, a committee that has helped fund many of the better recreational places in Minnesota.

Communities and citizens along rail-trails like the Munger realize the benefits that a trail provides and sometimes chose to work together on issues such as acquisition, development, linkages, and marketing. In 1992 the communities from Hinckley to Duluth formed the Munger Trail Towns Association and have already been invaluable to the Minnesota DNR in solving trail problems and improving the trail. They can be contacted at:

> Munger Trail Towns Association
> 205 Elm Avenue
> P. O. Box 110
> Moose Lake, MN 55767
> (218) 485-8836

Why not include some stamps or a dollar or two when requesting information?

M16 Willard Munger State Trail
Gateway Trail Segment
Minnesota Department of Natural Resources, Trails and Waterways

Primary: Asphalt. 🚶 🚲 🛷 ⛷ ♿

Secondary: Natural. ⛷ 🐴 (carriages allowed)

FYI: This trail's character changes abruptly at I-694. To the west is the city (plowed in the winter), and to the east the character is surprisingly rural.

Length: Primary: 16.9 miles.
  Secondary: 9.7 miles.

Fees: Great Minnesota Ski Pass. Daily parking fee of $3.00 at Pine Point Park Access.

Recommendation: Split the trail at the Oakdale access-head east to the more rural places, west back to town. For hiking, start at the Pine Point Park access and walk west. It's not far to the lakes and other pretty places.

FMI: Minnesota DNR Information Center

> St. Paul Area Chamber of Commerce
> 55 East Fifth Street
> #101
> St. Paul, MN 55101
> 612-223-5000

> Stillwater Area Chamber of Commerce
> 423 South Main Street
> Stillwater, MN 55082
> 612-439-7700

M16 Willard Munger
State Trail: Gateway
Trail Segment

0   1   2
Miles

General Trail Character: If trails were meant to connect people to places, especially urban dwellers to the country, the Gateway Trail does it. Opened in phases from 1991 to 1993, the trail's asphalt surface, flat grades, and varied scenery have made it instantly successful. From the Arlington Avenue access just north of the state capital to the fields and lakes of Washington County, the differences are dramatic. The route is that of a former Soo Line Railway from St. Paul to Wisconsin.

ST. PAUL (to Phalen-Keller Regional Park, 1.6 miles; to Oakdale, 7.1 miles)

St. Paul: Arlington Avenue and I-35E. Exit I-35E at Wheelock Parkway / Larpenteur Avenue. Go east on Wheelock 1 block, then south on Westminister, under a trestle to Arlington Avenue. Take a right, then one-half block to access on left. 🚗 🏠

Phalen-Keller Regional Park: At the north end of Lake Phalen (south side of Frost Avenue). The trail is on the north side of Frost, but a park trail goes under the road. 🚗

From the Arlington access the first 2 miles are a Tires to Trails Project: 3,300 shredded waste tires were blended into the asphalt. Unfortunately, the surface is popping loose, making in-line skating difficult. These 2 miles of neighborhoods, parks, and ponds are soon behind you, and the surface improves at the Phalen-Keller access. Bridges take you over the busier roads until you get parallel to Highway 36. This noisy section involves several well-marked but tricky street crossings, and parents should assist the kids. Fast food and other services are available.

OAKDALE (to Pine Point Park, 9.8 miles)

Oakdale: Off of State Highway 36, just west of I-694. From Highway 36 take Hadley Avenue south a few feet to 55th Street North. Turn left and follow 55th for .4 mile to well-marked access. 🚗 🏠

Note: There are other minor accesses between Oakdale and Pine Point Park, some with portable toilet facilities.

At I-694 the trail character changes abruptly. Now all the way to Pine Point Park you'll experience spacious housing developments, farms, birch woods, hollows, wetlands, and open places, with only a few road crossings. At times the primary treadway leaves the railroad bed, creating gentle curves and hills. Occasional benches and picnic tables invite lingering, and you will be surprised at how quiet this trail can be so close to the Twin Cities.

> **PINE POINT PARK**
> Washington County: Pine Point Park, on County Highway 55 (Norell Avenue), 3 miles north of State Highway 96. 🚗 🏕 🏠

Something Unique: Along Highway 36, in North St. Paul, is probably the world's largest artificial snowman.

More Trail: The DNR, Minnesota Department of Transportation, St. Paul Port Authority, and the City of St. Paul are cooperating in the planning and construction of a southerly 1.1 mile long extension. This should open in late 1996. Phalen-Keller Regional Park has 3 miles of trail around the lake. The Gateway Trail intersects with the **Burlington Northern Regional Trail.**

M17 Willard Munger State Trail

Hinckley Fire Trail Segment
Minnesota Department of Natural Resources, Trails and Waterways
Primary: Hinckley to Douglas Road: asphalt.
🚶 🚴 🛷 ♿ ⛷
FYI: A road route completes the trek into Carlton.
Length: 53 miles.
Fees: Great Minnesota Ski Pass.
Recommendation: Definitely do the bypass area between Finlayson and Rutledge. For more, keep going north.
FMI: Minnesota DNR Information Center
       Munger Trail Towns Association

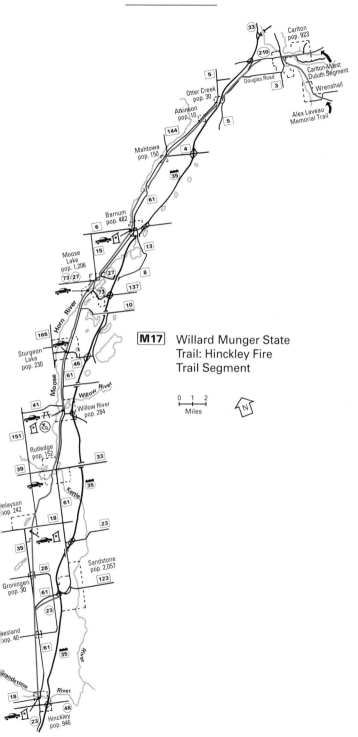

Carlton
pop. 923

(33)

(210)

5

Douglas Road

3

Carlton–West
Duluth Segment

Wrenshall

Otter Creek
pop. 30

Atkinson
pop. 10

5

Alex Laveau
Memorial Trail

144

4

Mahtowa
pop. 150

35

61

Barnum
pop. 482

6

15

13

Moose
Lake
pop. 1,206

(73)(27)

27

8

(73)

137

10

M17 Willard Munger State
Trail: Hinckley Fire
Trail Segment

165

Horn River

0   1   2
Miles

N

Sturgeon
Lake
pop. 230

46

61

Moose

Willow River

Willow River
pop. 284

41

151

Rutledge
pop. 152

39

33

35

Kettle

61

Finlayson
pop. 242

18

23

35

28

23

Sandstone
pop. 2,057

123

Groningen
pop. 30

61

23

esland
op. 40

61

35

River

randstone

River

18

48

23

Hinckley
pop. 946

General Trail Character: Your trip on this trail should start at the Hinckley Fire Museum. For $3.00 per adult you can explore the depot of the St. Paul and Duluth Railroad and watch the excellent video about the Hinckley Forest Fire of 1894. On the trail you are following the route hundreds of people took to escape this firestorm and the Moose Lake-Cloquet Fire of 1918. There's a trail-side fire memorial monument just north of Friesland, at Skunk Lake.

> **HINCKLEY (to Finlayson, 13 miles; to Rutledge, 5 miles; to Willow River, 5 miles)**
> **Hinckley:** Exit I-35 at State Highway 48. Go west to old Highway 61, then north to County Road 18, then left on 18 to access. �car 🏛
> **Finlayson:** East side of town just south of State Highway 18 at old depot. �car 🏛
> **Rutledge:** Off of County Road 37, just west of Highway 61. Street parking. �car

With a few exceptions, the trail is flat, straight, and fairly open, with mile after mile of woods, ponds with lilies, long views, and lots of wildness. You know you're part of a bigger trail system as the mileage markers start at 76 in Hinckley and increase as you go north. Between Finlayson and Rutledge is a two-mile piece of trail that is not on the right-of-way. It twists and turns, creating gentle hills along fields and forest as it completes its bypass. From Rutledge north the trail is frequently close to Highway 61 and is more open. All of it is well maintained.

> **WILLOW RIVER (to Sturgeon Lake, 4 miles; to Moose Lake, 9 miles; to Barnum, 5 miles)**
> **Willow River:** Willow River Community Park (marked from Highway 61). 🚗 🪑 🏛 ♿
> **Sturgeon Lake:** Off of County Road 46, just west of Highway 61. Street parking. 🚗
> **Moose Lake:** Just south of town on Highway 61. Marked. 🚗

At Willow River you can't miss the huge mural on the trailside shed. From there you can see the Willow River Mercantile Company, established in 1901, where you can buy anything from ice cream to TV's. North of town the trail crosses the Willow River. From there all the way to Moose Lake the trail is tight to Highway

61. In Moose Lake the trail detours off the right-of-way along 3rd Street and Birch Avenue, but a better bypass is scheduled to open in 1996.

> **BARNUM (to Township Road 5, 16 miles)**
> **Barnum:** West of town, on County Road 6
> (Main Street). 🚻 🏠
> **Note:** Trail passes through the very small
> towns of Mahtowa, Atkinson, Otter Creek.

This length closely parallels Highway 61. The towns are very small and offer few services.

More Trail: From the north end at Douglas Road it will be necessary to use the road to get into Carlton and on the **Carlton-West Duluth Trail** segment of the Munger. The north end of the **Alex Laveau Memorial Trail** (yet another Munger segment) can also be found in Carlton. On the north side of Moose Lake, the Trail goes under the **Soo Line Trail.** Seven miles north of Hinckley is a spur trail into Sandstone.

M18 Willard Munger State Trail

Carlton-West Duluth Trail Segment
Includes **Alex Laveau Memorial Trail**
Segment (M18-A)
Minnesota Department of Natural Resources,
Trails and Waterways
Primary: Asphalt. 🚶 🚲 ⛷ ♿ 🛶
Length: 14.5 miles.
Fees: Great Minnesota Ski Pass.
Recommendation: All of it. Or start at Carlton and go as far as you can. Mileage markers will help you keep track of the distance.
FMI: Minnesota DNR Information Center

Munger Trail Towns Association

Duluth Area Chamber of Commerce
118 East Superior Street
Duluth, MN 55802
218-722-4011

General Trail Character: Don't miss the dramatic views of the Duluth harbor and the rocky gorge of the St. Louis River near Jay Cooke State Park. Carlton

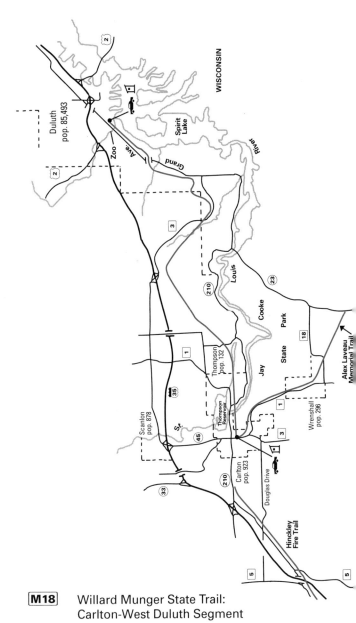

M18 Willard Munger State Trail:
Carlton-West Duluth Segment

M18-A Alex Laveau Memorial Trail

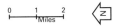

0 1 2
Miles

N

was and is still a significant railroad town. From here
the Northern Pacific Railroad began the drive to the
Pacific Ocean. Getting a train in and out of Duluth
was a challenge, and several companies used the
St. Louis corridor to do it. This trail segment occupies
what was once part of the Burlington Northern, the
result of a 1970 merger of the Northern Pacific with
three other companies.

CARLTON (to Duluth, 14.5 miles)
Carlton: From State Highway 210 in
downtown Carlton, turn south onto County
Road 1. Access in 1 block on left. 🚲 🏠

There are lengthy, steep grades from Lake Superior to
the uplands. Leave Carlton and in about five miles
you will notice the 9 mile-long descent toward West
Duluth. Be sure to keep that in mind if you have to
climb back up.

The gorge of the St. Louis River is only .5 mile from
the Carlton access and is worth a look over the bridge
railing. The river's water and gorge help define the
Thomson Hydroelectric Power facilities described as
the "great engineering feat of the 20th Century." Here
a dam-canal-pipeline system takes water to a power-
house for electrical generation. Much of the canal is
visible from the trail. In the first few miles you will
parallel Jay Cooke State Park and pass by the Hemlock Ravine State Natural Area.

Bring a camera for the rock cuts in the trails middle
portion and for the views from Bardon Peak Rest
Area of Spirit Lake and Wisconsin. Residential areas
appear as you enter West Duluth, and before you
know it, the grade has propelled you to the end.
Unfortunately, the trail suffers from tree-root damage,
creating a rough surface in places, inconvenient for
in-line skating. Funds for redevelopment have been
applied for.

DULUTH
Duluth: Nearly right across the street from the
Duluth Zoo and just off State Highway 23
(Grand Avenue). Look for signs on the high-
way. This puts it right behind the Willard
Munger Inn. 🚲 🏠

Something Unique: The gorge and rock cuts should not be missed.

More Trail: From Carlton, the **Alex Laveau Memorial Trail** segment takes you through Wrenshall to Highway 23 (about 6 miles). The highway can be used to return to Duluth. This creates 2 sides of a bikeable triangle with the third being the Munger Trail. The DNR owns the right-of-way from Highway 23 to the state line. The West Duluth end of the Munger is the beginning of Duluth's western **Waterfront Promenade** which may eventually connect with downtown Duluth. It could make extensive use of railroad right-of-way.

Minnesota –
Additional Rail-Trails

The rail trails listed here may be short, primarily of local interest, under development, or only a small part of a longer trail. They are listed by management structure.

ASSOCIATION

M-A   Central Lakes Trail, Avon to Fergus Falls
Length: 98.0 total, 98.0 Rail-Trails
Surface: Original ballast
Primary uses: 🚶 🚴 ⛷
FMI: Douglas Area Trails Association
      P.O. Box 112
      Alexandria, MN 56038
      612-834-2033
Comments: Former Burlington Northern (BN) corridor owned by the Minnesota Department of Transportation (MN DOT). The Douglas County to Fergus Falls section is the most developed.

**M-B   Minnewaska Snowmobile Trail, Starbuck to
        Villard**
Length: 25.0 total, 8.9 Rail-Trail
Surface: Original ballast
Primary uses: ⛷
FMI: see Central Lakes Trail
Comments: Right-of-way owned by MN DOT.

M-C   Superior Hiking Trail, Two Harbors to Canada
Length: 200.0 total, 3.0 Rail-Trail
Surface: Natural
Primary uses: 🚶
FMI: Superior Hiking Trail Association
      P.O. Box 4
      731 7th Avenue
      Two Harbors, MN 55616
      218-834-2700
Comments: This lengthy hiking trail follows the ridge above the North Shore of Lake Superior.

CITY

M-D   Burlington Northern Regional Trail, St. Paul
Length: 3.0 total, 3.0 Rail-Trail
Surface: Asphalt
Primary uses: 🚶 🚴 ⛷ ♿
FMI: City of St. Paul Parks and Recreation
      300 City Hall Annex
      St. Paul, MN 55102
      612-266-6400
Comments: Connects downtown with points north via the Ramsey County portion of this same trail.

**M-E   Cedar Lake Trail, Minneapolis (downtown) to
         St. Louis Park**
Length: 4.3 total, 4.3 Rail-Trail
Surface: Asphalt
Primary uses: 🏃 🚲 ⛷ ♿
FMI: Minneapolis Park and Recreation Board
        200 Grain Exchange
        400 South 4th Street
        Minneapolis, MN 55415
        612-661-4826
Comments: Commuter route with multiple separate
treadways.

**M-F   Duluth, Winnipeg, and Pacific Railway Line,
         Near Carlton to West Duluth**
Length: 10.5 total, 10.5 Rail-Trail
Surface: Original ballast
Primary uses: 🏃 🚵 🐴
FMI: Duluth Parks and Recreation
        City Hall
        411 West First Street
        Duluth, MN 55802
        218-723-3337
Comments: Parallel, but higher up the hill, to the Munger
Trail (Carlton - West Duluth Segment). Has Minnesota's
only trail tunnel which is 480' long and sharply curved.

M-G   Loop Trail System, Minnetonka
Length: 40.0 total, 1.0 Rail-Trail
Surface: Asphalt / crushed rock
Primary uses: 🏃 🚲 ♿
FMI: City of Minnetonka
        Trail Coordinator
        14600 Minnetonka Boulevard
        Minnetonka, MN 55345
        612-93T-RAIL
Comments: This system connects to the Luce Line State Trail
and incorporates parts of the Hennepin Parks Light Rail
Transit Trails. The system also includes one-half mile of
trail on old trolley right-of-way and a second one-half mile
length of old right-of-way.

**M-H   Midtown Greenway, Minneapolis to St. Paul
         city limits**
Length: 4.5 total, 4.5 Rail-Trail
Surface: Asphalt
Primary uses: 🏃 🚲 ⛷ ♿
FMI: Minneapolis Public Works Department
        350 South Fifth Street
        City Hall, Room 203
        Minneapolis, MN 55415
Comments: Under development. Generally parallels Lake
Street but one block north. Will offer non-stop travel from
the Chain of Lakes to the Mississippi River.

M-I **St. Croix Bikeway, Afton to Lakeland,**
I-94/12 bridge to Hudson, WI
Length: 3.4 total, 2.2 Rail-Trail
Surface: Asphalt
Primary uses: 🚶 🚲 🛶 ♿ ⛷
FMI: City of Lakeland
    690 Quinnell Avenue North
    Lakeland, MN 55043
    612-436-4430
Comments: Most of this trail is parallel to Highway 95.
Crosses the St. Croix River.

M-J **Waterfront Promenade, Duluth**
Length: 2.5 total, 1.0 (estimate) Rail-Trail
Surface: Asphalt
Primary uses: 🚶 🚲 🛶 ♿
FMI: City of Duluth Parks and Recreatioin
    330 City Hall
    411 West 1st Street
    Duluth, MN 55802
    218-723-3337
Comments: An ambitious project which may end up using a
considerable amount railroad right of way.

M-K **West Mankato Trail, Mankato**
Length: 1.5 total, 1.5 Rail-Trail
Surface: Asphalt
Primary uses: 🚶 🚲 🛶 ♿
FMI: City of Mankato
    Parks and Forestry Department
    P.O. Box 3368
    Mankato, MN 56002
    507-387-8650
Comments: Connects to the Red Jacket Trail.

M-L **West River Parkway, Minneapolis**
Length: 6.3 total, 1.25 Rail-Trail
Surface: Asphalt
Primary uses: 🚶 🚲 🛶 ♿
FMI: see Cedar Lake Trail
Comments: Follows the Mississippi River from downtown to
Minnehaha Falls.

COUNTY

M-M **Big Rivers Regional Trail, Mendota**
Length: 4.2 total, 4.2 Rail-Trail
Surface: Asphalt
Primary uses: 🚶 🚲 🛶 ♿
FMI: Dakota County Parks
    500 127th Street East
    Hastings, MN 55033
    612-438-4660
Comments: A link in the plan to connect trails along the Min-
nesota and Mississippi Rivers. Right-of-way leased from
MnDOT.

M-N **Burlington Northern Regional Trail,**
Maplewood
Length: 2.0 total, 2.0 Rail-Trail
Surface: Asphalt
Primary uses: 🚶 🚴 ⛷ ♿
FMI: Ramsey County Parks
     2015 N. Van Dyke St.
     Maplewood, MN 55109
     612-777-1707
Comments: Intersects with Munger State Trail, Gateway Segment.

M-O **Hardwood Creek Trail, Hugo to Chisago County**
Line
Length: 9.5 total, 9.5 Rail-Trail
Surface: Asphalt
Primary uses: 🚶 🚴 ⛷ 🐎 ♿
FMI: Washington County Public Works / Parks
     11660 Myeron Road West
     Stillwater, MN 55082
Comments: Under development. Connects to North Branch
via Sunrise Prairie Trail.

M-P **Red Jacket Trail, Mankato to near Rapidan**
Length: 5.6 total, 5.6 Rail-Trail
Surface: Crushed rock
Primary uses: 🚶 🚴 🏇 ♿
FMI: Blue Earth County Public Works Department
     35 Map Drive
     Mankato, MN 56001
Comments: Under development. Travels a scenic wooded valley. Asphalt surface planned for 1997.

M-Q **Sunrise Prairie Trail, Washington County line to**
North Branch
Length: 15.5 total, 15.5 Rail-Trail
Surface: Asphalt
Primary uses: 🚶 🚴 ⛷ 🐎 ♿
FMI: Chisago County Parks Department
     38694 Tanger Drive
     North Branch, MN 55056
     612-257-2982
Comments: Connects to Hugo via Hardwood Creek Trail.
May open in 1996.

MULTI-COUNTY

M-R **Mesabi Range Trail, Grand Rapids to Ely**
Length: 132.0 total
Surface: Asphalt
Primary uses: 🚶 🚴 ⛷ ♿ 🐎 🐕 dogsled
FMI: Itasca County Park Department
     123 NE 4th Street
     Grand Rapis, MN 55744
     218-327-2855
Comments: In the planning stages and portions under development. Route not entirely determined but likely to make
considerable use of railroad corridors.

M-S   Soo Line Trail, Northern Route, Moose Lake through Chippewa National Forest

Length: 112.0 total, 112.0 Rail-Trail
Surface: Original ballast
Primary uses: 🚶 🚵 🏇 some 🚴 and 🐾
FMI: Chippewa National Forest
        Route 3, Box 219
        Cass Lake, MN 56635
        218-335-2283
Comments: Travels remote country and is owned by the counties it traverses.

M-T   Soo Line Trail, Southern Route

Length: 114.0 total, 114.0 Rail-Trail
Surface: Original ballast
Primary uses: 🚶 🚵 🏇 some 🚴 and 🐾
FMI: Moose Lake Area Chamber of Commerce
        P.O. Box 110
        Moose Lake, MN 55767
        218-485-4145, 800-635-3680
Comments: Joins the Northern Route at Moose Lake. Owned by the counties it traverses. Several miles near Onamia now asphalt surfaced.

MINNESOTA DEPARTMENT OF NATURAL RESOURCES

M-U   Arrowhead State Trail, Tower to South International Falls

Length: 128 total, 30.0 Rail-Trail
Surface: Original ballast
Primary uses: 🚶 🏇
FMI: Minnesota DNR
        Information Center
Comments: Remote country.

M-V   Banning State Park Quarry and Spur Trails, Sandstone

Length: 2.0 total, 2.0 Rail-Trail
Surface: Natural
Primary uses: 🚶 🚵
FMI: Minnesota DNR
        Information Center
Comments: Much of the history of this park involves railroads and quarries. Near the spectacular Kettle River.

M-W   Blue Ox Trail, Bemidji to International Falls

Length: 105.0 total, 105.0 Rail-Trail
Surface: Original ballast
Primary uses: 🚶 🚲 🏇
FMI: Minnesota DNR
        Information Center
Comments: Former BN railroad. Owned by MN DOT and operated by the DNR under a limited use permit. Parallel to Highway 71.

M-X   Casey Jones State Trail, Pipestone to near Lake Wilson
Length: 13.5 total, 13.5 Rail-Trail
Surface: Original ballast
Primary uses: 🚶 🚴 🐎
FMI: Minnesota DNR
    Information Center
Comments: In two segments, one of 12 miles and another of 1.5 miles.

M-Y   Circle L Trail, East of Big Fork
Length: 22.5 total, 2.0 Rail-Trail
Surface: Natural
Primary uses: 🚴
FMI: Minnesota DNR
    Information Center
Comments: Remote country.

M-Z   Circle T Trail, West of Togo
Length: 39.5 total, 3.0 Rail-Trail
Surface: Natural
Primary uses: 🚴
FMI: Minnesota DNR
    Information Center
Comments: Connects to the Circle L Trail

M-AA   Cloquet to Saginaw, Cloquet to Saginaw
Length: 7.0 total, 7.0 Rail-Trail
Surface: Original ballast
Primary uses: 🚶
FMI: Minnesota DNR
    Information Center
Comments: Recreation plan in progress.

M-AB   Gandy Dancer Trail, Danbury to state line
Length: 31.0 total, 31.0 Rail-Trail
Surface: Original ballast
Primary uses: 🚴 🛷
FMI: Minnesota DNR
    Information Center
Comments: Connects to the Wisconsin portion of the Gandy Dancer. Serves as a logging haul road also.

M-AC   Goodhue–Pioneer Trail, Zumbrota to Red Wing
Length: 40.0 total, 9.0 Rail-Trail
Surface: Natural
Primary uses: 🚶 🚴
FMI: Minnesota DNR
    Information Center
Comments: This trail is envisioned to connect the Douglas State Trail to Cannon Valley Trail via Mazeppa, Zumbrota, and Goodhue. Would incorporate the Hay Creek Management Unit Trail.

**M-AD   Minnehaha Trail, From Minneapolis's
        Minnehaha Park to Fort Snelling State Park**
Length: 2.0 total, 2.0 Rail-Trail
Surface: Asphalt
Primary uses: 🚶 🚴 🛷 ♿
FMI: Minnesota DNR
        Information Center
Comments: Travels below the stone ramparts of Fort
Snelling. Connects to other trails.

M-AE   Pengilly to Alborn, Pengilly to Alborn
Length: 40.0 total, 40.0 Rail-Trail
Surface: Original ballast
Primary uses: 🚶 🐎 🐕
FMI: Minnesota DNR
        Information Center
Comments: Very remote and pretty.

**M-AF   Racine Prairie State Natural Area, Along
        Highway 63, 2 miles north of Racine**
Length: 0.5 total, 0.5 Rail-Trail
Surface: Natural
Primary uses: 🚶
FMI: Minnesota DNR
        Information Center
Comments: A rare example of the Southeastern Tallgrass
Prairie.

**M-AG   Shooting Star Prairie State Natural Area, Along
        Highway 56, 4 miles west of LeRoy**
Length: 0.7 total, 0.7 Rail-Trail
Surface: Natural
Primary uses: 🚶
FMI: Minnesota DNR
        Information Center
Comments: A mixed woods and prairie resource. Once part
of the Milwaukee Road system.

M-AH   Taconite State Trail, Grand Rapids to Ely
Length: 165.0 total, 21.0 Rail-Trail
Surface: Original ballast
Primary uses: 🚶 🐎
FMI: Minnesota DNR
        Information Center
Comments: A very long and remote trail.

**M-AI   Wild Indigo State Natural Area, Ramsey to
        Dexter**
Length: 12.5 total, 12.5 Rail-Trail
Surface: Natural
Primary uses: 🚶
FMI: Minnesota DNR
        Information Center
Comments: This area occupies part of one of oldest railroads
in the state (1870) which ended up as part of the Milwaukee
Road. Contains at least 340 plant species.

4:
Rail-Trails of Western Wisconsin

At the latest count Wisconsin boasted 47 rail-trails and some of the better ones are in Western Wisconsin. In the area covered by this guide you will find 15 rail-trails described and another 12 mentioned. The Wisconsin Department of Natural Resources once established and operated most rail-trails, but this is beginning to change because railroad abandonments continue so fast as to preclude state involvement in all of them.

Rail-trails operated by the Wisconsin DNR are classified either as State Park Trails or State Recreation Trails. In general, State Park Trails are non-motorized, and no hunting is allowed. State Recreation Trails may allow some motorized use and hunting but not necessarily on the entire trail. A State Trail Admission Pass is required to access DNR rail-trails if you are bicycling or skiing and age 16 or older. Rates are: daily pass–$3.00, annual–$10.00. Self-registration stations are conveniently located at most major accesses, and at times attendants may be present.

Rail-Trails of Western Wisconsin

Described Trails

Trail Number	Name
W1	Buffalo River State Park Trail
W2	Cheese Country Recreational Trail
W3	Chippewa River State Recreation Trail
W3-A	Eau Claire City Trail
W4	Elroy–Sparta State Park Trail
W5	Gandy Dancer Trail
W6	Great River State Park Trail
W7	LaCrosse River State Park Trail
W8	Military Ridge State Park Trail
W9	Omaha Trail
W10	Pecatonica State Park Trail
W11	Red Cedar State Park Trail
W11-A	City of Menomonie Trail
W12	Sugar River State Trail
W13	The 400 State Trail

Additional Trails

Trail Number	Name
W-A	Pine River Trail
W-B	The Pine Line
W-C	Oliver–Wrenshall Grade Trail
W-D	Soo Line Trail
W-E	South Shore / Battleaxe / #63
W-F	Woodville Trail
W-G	Cattail Trail
W-H	Tri-County Corridor
W-I	Old Abe State Recreation Trail
W-J	Tuscobia State Trail

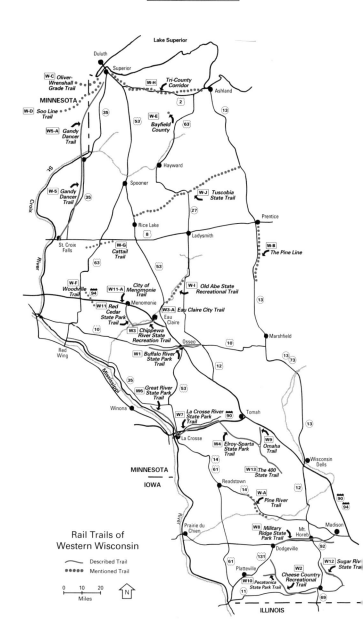

Rail Trails of
Western Wisconsin

—— Described Trail
••••• Mentioned Trail

0   10   20
Miles

N

W1 Buffalo River State Park Trail

Wisconsin Department of Natural Resources
Primary: Original ballast (some crushed rock).
🚶 🚵

⛷ 🐕 (December 1–April 30)
🐕 🐎 (May 15–October 31)
FYI: The trail is closed March 2–May 15 and
November 1–November 30.
Length: 36.4 miles.
Fees: Trail Admission Pass.
Recommendation: Mondovi east 1 mile.
Price to Fairchild (4 miles) or Strum to Osseo
(8 miles).
FMI: Buffalo River State Park Trail
      1300 West Clairemont Avenue
      P. O. Box 4001
      Eau Claire, WI 54702
      715-839-1607

      Eau Claire Area Chamber of Commerce
      505 Dewey Street South
      Eau Claire, WI 54701
      715-834-1204

General Trail Character: The Buffalo River State Trail
parallels Highway 10 nearly its whole length, but it's
not dull. You'll find a varied landscape of hills, floodplain, prairie, oak savanna, pine plantations, fields,
and wetlands. There are some wild and quiet places.
The right-of-way was finished in 1890 by the Fairchild
and Mississippi Railway, then sold the next year to the
Chicago, St. Paul, Milwaukee, and Omaha Railroad.
It was abandoned by the Chicago and North Western
Transportation Company in 1975. While in service, it
provided daily mixed freight and commercial service.

> ### MONDOVI (to Eleva, 11.5 miles; to Strum, 4 miles)
> **Mondovi:** East side of town. At intersection
> of U. S. Highway 10 and State Highway 37 go
> south on Marten Road to trail. 🚙
> **Eleva:** Trail crosses State Highway 93 south
> side of town, just north of the Buffalo River.
> No developed access. Street parking. 🚙

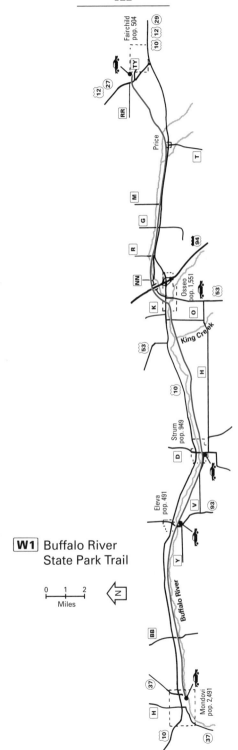

W1 Buffalo River
State Park Trail

The special qualities of the Buffalo River start immediately from Mondovi and last about a mile before
the trail gets tight to Highway 10 almost to Eleva. At
Eleva is the first of four river crossings, and the next
4 miles to Strum offer a wilder experience.

STRUM (to Osseo, 8 miles)
Strum: Downtown. 🚗

Strum is a small Wisconsin town with a nice lake on
the north side. You have to leave the trail at Highway
D in the middle of town to find it. Along the way is
Woodland Park with water and toilets. The trail to
Osseo is wilder, equally open and wooded, with few
reminders of civilization. You will pass through the
King Creek Public Hunting and Fishing Area.

OSSEO (to Fairchild, 13 miles)
Osseo: West side of town. No developed
access. Street parking. 🚗

Roads are again parallel from Osseo to Price, an un-
incorporated wide spot on the trail. Mileage markers
will help you keep track of this 9-mile stretch. The
final 4 miles to Fairchild are well wooded, offering
great views of strange looking hills and even a tamarack bog or two. Fairchild is small and old. You have
to go into town farther than the access to see much
of it.

FAIRCHILD
Fairchild: Just off of Highway 27 / 12 along
County Road YY, 1 mile north of Highway
10. Signed from YY. 🚗

Something Unique: Explore Price (it won't take long).
The white steepled Price Evangelical Lutheran Church
is eloquent.

W2 Cheese Country Recreational Trail

Tri-County Rails-to-Trails Commission
Primary: Crushed rock.December 1–March 30
🏃 🛷 🐕
April 1–November 15 🏃 🚵 🐕 🐎
FYI: Trail is closed to vehicles November 15–
December 1. Motorized vehicles yield to non-
motorized uses.
Length: 47 miles.
Fees: State registration of vehicles or $6.00
annual Trail Sticker. Bicyclists aged 18 and
older: also $6.00 annual. Available locally.
Recommendation: Mineral Point to Darlington
(15 miles). Cadiz Springs State Recreation Area.
FMI: Cheese Country Recreational Trail
          Project Coordinator
          Ag Center
          Darlington, WI 53530
          608-776-4830

          Lafayette County Tourism Information
          c/o University of Wisconsin Extension
          Office
          Courthouse
          Darlington, WI 53530
          (608)-776-4820

General Trail Character: The Cheese Country Recreational Trail takes the multi-use concept further than
about any other trail, as motorized recreational vehicles mix with horses, bicyclists, and pedestrians. This
Milwaukee Road line paralleled the Pecatonica River,
starting in 1853, as a result of the discovery of lead in
the region. The last train was in February, 1985 and
the trail opened in late 1992. Recreational use is considered temporary in the event rail service is ever
again feasible. A trail of this length exposes the trav-
eler to a wide variety of habitats and scenery with the
transitions coming slowly. The experience is much
like what a nice country road offers.

MINERAL POINT (to Calamine, 9 miles)

Mineral Point: Below downtown, on Old Darlington Road just east of Commerce Street. 🚗

Mineral Springs, with its great historic downtown,
could be explored all day. When you finally get on the

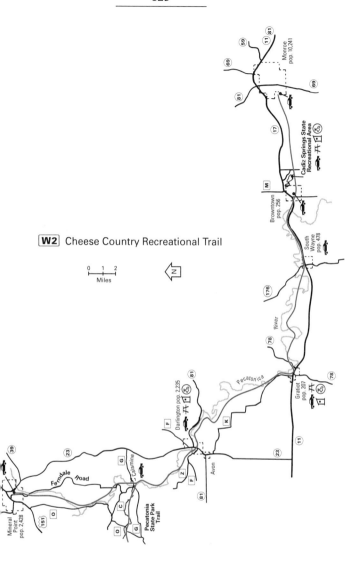

W2 Cheese Country Recreational Trail

trail, you will be heading down a scenic valley that soon opens up into a remote, broad landscape of pastures, fields, and woods.

CALAMINE (to Darlington, 6 miles)
Calamine: West side of town, along County Road G, across from old fertilizer plant.

At Calamine, 200 yards south of the access, is the barely marked intersection with the Wisconsin DNR

Pecatonica State Park Trail. Both of these trails have been severely impacted by floods, putting the managing agencies in a constant repair cycle. As you head toward Darlington, you'll find the Pecatonica River, fields, and occasional forest.

DARLINGTON (to Gratiot, 12 miles: to South Wayne, 8 miles: to Browntown, 4 miles)

Darlington: Trail crosses downtown by Coop Station (hard to see). Park behind station at Depot Museum. 🚗 🅰 🄵 ♿

Gratiot: City Park behind The Nugget Restaurant. 🚗 🅰 🄵 ♿

South Wayne: Center of town. Look for signs. 🚗

At Darlington the trail takes you right through downtown, a place you wouldn't want to miss anyway. From here all the way to South Wayne there are few adjacent roads, and you will see the rich Wisconsin countryside of fields, dairy farms, and common rural wildlife. At Gratiot is a dilapidated old depot. Cheese Country has 57 bridges, the longest of which is 440 feet over the Pecatonica River west of Browntown. Most trestles were planked and railed by local snowmobile and ATV clubs.

BROWNTOWN (to Cadiz Springs State Recreation Area, 3 miles; to Monroe, 5 miles)

Browntown: Small access on County Road M. 🚗

Cadiz Springs State Recreation Area: Trail is south boundary of Area. Connection not wheelchair accessible. 🚗 🅰 🄵 ♿

East of Browntown is the Cadiz Springs State Recreation Area with two beautiful lakes, fine hiking trails, and the usual park amenities. You have to climb down from the elevated trail to get into the area. The final miles to Monroe are moderate to well-wooded through a hilly landscape.

MONROE

Monroe: Southwest side of town. From State Highway 11 go south on 4th Avenue West (by Hardees) .3 mile to "T". Then right to access. 🚗

Something Unique: When in Darlington, visit the 1905 Lafayette County Courthouse at the high end of downtown. The limestone, marble, and mahogany are striking.

More Trail: **Pecatonica State Park Trail** at Calamine, also operated by the Tri-County Rails-to-Trails Commission but owned by the Wisconsin Department of Natural Resources.

W3   Chippewa River State Recreation Trail

Includes **Eau Claire City Trail** (W3-A)
Wisconsin Department of Natural Resources
City of Eau Claire
Primary:
Red Cedar Trail to Highway 85 — asphalt emulsion. 🚶 🚴 🏃 ♿ 🛶
Highway 85 to Eau Claire — asphalt. 🚶 🚴 🏃 🛶 ♿
Length: 23 miles.
Fees: Trail Admission Pass (DNR portion only).
Recommendation: From Eau Claire to the Highway 85 access (7 miles).
FMI: Wisconsin DNR
      1300 West Clairemont Avenue
      P. O. Box 4001
      Eau Claire, WI 54702
      715-839-1607

      Eau Claire Area Convention and
      Visitors Bureau
      2127 Brackett Avenue
      Eau Claire, WI 54701
      715-839-2919
      800-344-FUNN

General Trail Character: Through the Chippewa River valley five trails will merge eventually to create a 70-mile route. The Red Cedar, Chippewa River, and Eau Claire City trails make the Menomonie to Eau Claire connection. Trail is proposed to occupy the Wisconsin Central Short Line track from Eau Claire to Chippewa

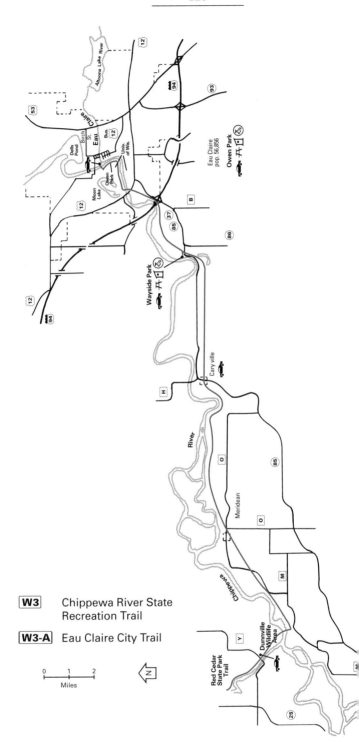

W3 Chippewa River State Recreation Trail

W3-A Eau Claire City Trail

Falls. The existing but undeveloped Old Abe travels
20 miles from Chippewa Falls to Cornell and would
anchor the northeastern end of the system. The Chippewa River State Recreation Trail has distinct character changes as it parallels the wide Chippewa River.
Lumbering was the major reason for this line. Con-
structed in the 1870's, it connected Menomonie and
Eau Claire with the Mississippi River. For most of
its existence it was part of the Chicago, Milwaukee,
St. Paul and Pacific Railroad. The Chippewa Trail
connects to the Red Cedar Trails 800-foot long bridge
over the Chippewa River.

RED CEDAR TRAIL (to Meridean, 5 miles; to Caryville; 10 miles)

Red Cedar State Park Trail: The southern
end of the Red Cedar connects to the west end
of the Chippewa. No facilities.

This ten-mile stretch is the wilder portion of trail. See-
ing a Bald Eagle is not uncommon. Meridean is about
as quiet as a small town can get. The asphalt-emulsion
surface is uncommon to Midwestern trails but provides a surface that rates somewhere between crushed
rock and asphalt.

CARYVILLE (to Highway 85 Wayside Park, 5 miles)

Caryville: North side of town at crossing with
State Highway 85, next to Luer's Grocery. 🚗

At Caryville you will find a well developed treadway
through a mostly wide open agricultural landscape.
Light woods provide some relief, and in between are
many prairie species. At the Highway 85 underpass
the surface changes to 10 foot asphalt. A paved spur
leads into the Wayside Park.

HIGHWAY 85 WAYSIDE PARK (to Eau Claire, 8 miles)

Highway 85 Wayside Park: West of Eau
Claire along Highway 85, 2 miles west of I-94.
🚗 ⛱ 🏠 ♿

Not far from the Wayside Park the trail leaves the
right-of-way for a couple of miles and follows the
Chippewa River. This had its disadvantages during the
1993 floods, but the forest and birds of the floodplain
are agreeable. The scenery becomes increasingly
urban as you head east. I-94 and U. S. Highway 12

crossings come next before you reach the fabulous old iron bridge that takes you over the river and into town. Spiral around the end of the bridge, and you're headed upstream along a well-designed city trail, weaving its way through the University of Wisconsin campus, city parks, and commercial areas. Eventually you cross the river again on another iron trestle.

EAU CLAIRE

Eau Claire: Pick up City Trail from virtually anywhere along the west bank of the Chippewa River, or the University of Wisconsin-Eau Claire campus at 1st Avenue and Water Street. 🚶 🏕 🅿️ ♿

Something Unique: If you like impressive railroad trestles this trail has them.

More Trail: To the west is the **Red Cedar State Park Trail,** and to the east may someday be the Urban Trail to Chippewa Falls.

W4 Elroy-Sparta State Park Trail

Wisconsin Department of Natural Resources
Primary: Crushed rock. 🚶 🚴 ♿ ⛷️
FYI: Walk single file in the tunnels. Tunnels are closed in the winter. Driver shuttle service available for a fee. Contact Trail Headquarters at Kendall.
Length: 32 miles.
Fees: Trail Admission Pass.
Recommendation: The qualities of this trail are so well distributed that doing it all must be considered. For a shorter trip try Sparta to Wilton or vice versa (19 miles). Or park where Highway 71 and the trail cross, 4 miles north of Norwalk (look carefully), and head east on the trail. You can reach the Summit Rest Area through Tunnel #3 in 1.5 miles.
FMI: Elroy–Sparta State Park Trail
      Headquarters
      P. O. Box 297
      Kendall, WI 54638
      608-463-7109

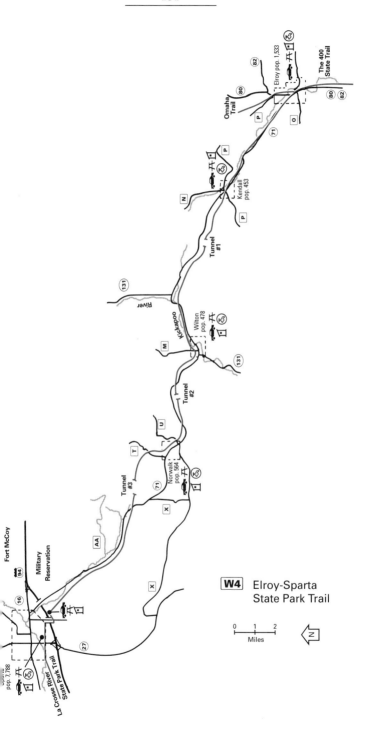

W4 Elroy-Sparta
State Park Trail

Sparta Area Chamber of Commerce
111 Milwaukee Street
Sparta, WI 54656
608-269-4123
800-354-BIKE

General Trail Character: The Great River, La Crosse,
Elroy–Sparta, The 400, and Omaha trails now connect for a virtually uninterrupted 112-mile experience.
Tunnels and towns have made the Elroy–Sparta trail
famous. The unglaciated southwestern Wisconsin
scenery helps too. It is one of the country's oldest rail-
trails, having been purchased by the Wisconsin DNR
in 1965 for $12,000 (probably the best rail-trail bar-
gain anywhere). From 1873 to 1911 about 6 passenger
and 40 to 50 freight trains a day used this Chicago and
North Western line between Madison and Winona.
Passenger service was discontinued in 1953, and the
last train ran in 1964. The longest of the three tunnels
is 3,810 feet and you should take a flashlight to find
your way through. The host communities are very
hospitable to trail visitors.

ELROY (to Kendall, 6 miles; to Wilton, 9 miles)
Elroy: The Commons (downtown park) right
along State Highway 71. 🚲 🚻 🏚 ♿
Kendall: At Trail Headquarters Depot downtown. Well marked. 🚲 🚻 🏚 ♿

Elroy has the distinction of being a trail hub with 3
radiating from the downtown Commons Park. To the
south is the 400 State Trail, to the north the Omaha
Trail, and to the northwest the Elroy–Sparta Trail.
Toward Kendall the trail begins with wooded hills,
farms, and is tight to Highway 71. In Kendall the
restored depot with handicapped accessible facilities,
serves as a seasonal trail headquarters with concessions
and informative historical displays. From Kendall
northwest, not much of the trail is level as you are
constantly gently ascending to a tunnel or descending.
Tunnels #1 and #2 are .25 mile long and provide natural (but wet) air-conditioned relief from hot summer
days. The scenery of wooded hills and farms returns
again, and the trail parallels Highway 71 to the midway town of Wilton.

WILTON *(to Norwalk, 6 miles; to Sparta, 13 miles)*
Wilton: Just north of downtown. 🚗 🏕 🏠 ♿
Norwalk: Village Park just east of downtown
Main Street. 🚗 🏕 🏠 ♿

Wilton is a friendly community that advertises itself
as the heart of the trail. Its midpoint location makes it
a great place to start. Tunnel #2 must be negotiated to
get to Norwalk, the "Gateway to the Tunnels." From
here the four miles to Tunnel #3 (the long one) leaves
Highway 71, and you begin the climb to Summit Rest
Area. As exciting as it is to enter Tunnel #3, be sure to
linger at the rest area to enjoy the railroad-history displays and the camaraderie of other trail users. You
may want to put on a light jacket for the wet .75-mile
tunnel. The final stretch to Sparta again parallels
Highway 71, ending at a well-developed access just
south of I-90. A signed bike route takes you into town,
where you can connect with the La Crosse River State
Trail.

SPARTA
Sparta: At depot. From I-90 take State High-
way 27 north just into town. Depot on right.
Well marked. 🚗 🏕 🏠 ♿
Rural: Southeast of town, south of I-90 off of
Johns Street. Well marked. 🚗

Something Unique: Tunnels and towns. All of them!
The Wilton Lions Club serves a pancake breakfast in
the Municipal Park on Sunday mornings from June to
September.

More Trail: From Sparta is the **La Crosse River Sate
Park Trail.** From Elroy is the **400 State Trail** and
Omaha Trail.

W5 Gandy Dancer Trail

Wisconsin: Burnett, Polk, Douglas counties
Minnesota: Minnesota Department of Natural Resources, Forestry

Primary: St. Croix Falls to Danbury: limestone screenings. 🚶 🚴 🛷

(ATV's and snowmobiles allowed December 15–March 31, when snow is 6 inches or deeper).

Minnesota portion: original ballast. 🚶 🚴 🛷 🛷 🛷 🐎

(summer only — carriages allowed; some other motorized uses allowed).

Wisconsin, remainder: original ballast. 🚶 🚴 🛷

FYI: One of three interstate trails between Minnesota and Wisconsin.

Length: 95.4 miles (includes 31 miles of Minnesota trail).

Fees: St. Croix Falls to Danbury, for bicycles only: $10 annual, $3.00 daily.

Recommendation: Danbury to the St. Croix River bridge (.5 mile). Continue into Minnesota's 44,500-acre St. Croix State Forest for a sense of the northern half of this trail. In the southern half try, Danbury to Webster (10 miles).

FMI: Polk County Information Center
      Highway 35 & 8
      St. Croix Falls, WI
      1-800-222-7655

      Siren Area Chamber of Commerce
      24049 1st Avenue North
      Siren, WI 54872
      715-349-2273

General Trail Character: The Gandy Dancer crosses the state line at Danbury, Wisconsin, and again south of Superior, connecting the Wisconsin cities of St. Croix Falls and Superior via Minnesota. The project got started in 1989, when the governors of Minnesota and Wisconsin signed a resolution of endorsement for an interstate rail-trail. In 1986 the Soo Line Railroad abandoned this lengthy stretch, and the tracks and ties were removed in 1990. The term "gandy dancer" has

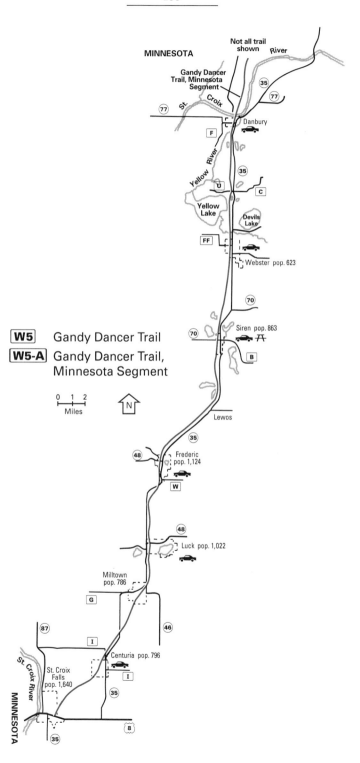

W5 Gandy Dancer Trail

W5-A Gandy Dancer Trail, Minnesota Segment

its origins from the now defunct Gandy Manufacturing Company, which made tools used by railroad workers. Dancer refers to the rhythmic movements of men using the tools. South of Danbury this trail, often visible from Highway 35, connects 8 evenly spaced towns and travels through a semi-open country of lakes, woods, and farms. To the north it's wild, wet, and remote, requiring independence and preparation.

ST. CROIX (to Danbury via 7 small towns, 49.5 miles)
St. Croix Falls: One mile extension to Polk County Tourism Office at Highways 35/8 is planned by summer, 1996.
Centuria: Downtown. ▰
Milltown: West side of Business District. Street Parking. ▰
Luck: .3 mile west of Highway 35 on East 48th Street. ▰
Frederic: Two blocks west of Highway 35 on State Highway 48. ▰
Siren: West side of Business District at City Park. ▰ ⚘
Webster: 3 blocks west of Highway 35 on Main Street. ▰

The trail from St. Croix Falls north to Centuria diagonals across the landscape straight and level, then parallels Highway 35 all the way to Danbury. There are enough trees to keep you moderately shaded. The transition from agriculture to woods happens slowly as you pass the nearly evenly spaced small towns. Streams and small lakes become more common, all tributaries to the St. Croix River. Lumbering, past and present, is important to the region's character.

DANBURY (to Superior, 45.9 miles)
Danbury: One block west of Highway 35 on State Highway 77. ▰
Markville: Trail crosses County Road 25 on west side of town. Road parking. ▰
Superior: South of town on County Road C, 2 blocks west of Highway 35. Not convenient. Road parking. ▰

Danbury, where you cross the river and state line, has a fantastic view from the bridge. From here to Superior is a wooded place with very few services. Minnesota's section of 30.4 miles is bordered mostly by the St. Croix and Nemadji state forests and County Road 31 for parts of the middle. Motorized recreation is the dominant use, and portions of the trail will be used as logging roads. Detours may be encountered.

Something Unique: The bridge over the St. Croix River, a federally designated wild and scenic place.

W6 Great River State Park Trail

Wisconsin Department of Natural Resources
Primary: Crushed rock. ⅍ ⚲ ⚐ (between Onalaska and Midway) ⚹ ⚓ (Onalaska to Perrot State Park)
Length: 24 miles.
Fees: Trail Admission Pass.
Recommendation: This whole trail is not hard to do. The gentle grade from Marshland down to Onalaska helps a little.
FMI: Great River State Park Trail
Route 1, Box 407
Trempealeau, WI 54661
608-534-6409

Onalaska Center for Commerce & Tourism
800 Oak Forest Drive
Onalaska, WI 54650
608-781-9570

General Trail Character: This trail follows a great river and valley. You will flow along the extensive backwaters of the Mississippi, crossing marshes and tributaries on 18 bridges, including the braided Black River. The La Crosse, Trempealeau, and Prescott Railroad started in 1857 connecting the cities of its name. This line ended up as part of the Chicago and North Western system and was abandoned in 1967. Burlington Northern active tracks still parallel this old line but usually at some distance. The wide waters, Minnesota and Wisconsin bluffs, and foreground prairie color combine to make a memorable trail experience.

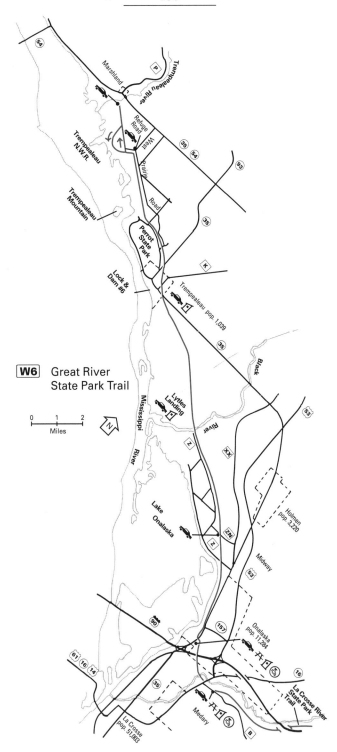

W6 Great River
State Park Trail

0   1   2
Miles

N

Marshland

Trempealeau River

P

Refuge Road

West Prairie Road

Trempealeau N.W.R.

Trempealeau Mountain

35

54

93

Perrot State Park

Lock & Dam #6

K

Trempealeau pop. 1,039

35

Black

53

Mississippi River

Lytles Landing

River

Z

XX

ZN

Z

Lake Onalaska

Holmen pop. 3,220

Midway

53

90

157

Onalaska pop. 11,284

61 16 14

35

Medary

La Crosse pop. 51,003

La Crosse River State Park Trail

16

B

ONALASKA (to Midway, 3.2 miles; to Lytles Landing, 5.4 miles; to Trempealeau, 5.4 miles)

Onalaska: Onalaska Center for Commerce and Tourism, right along State Highway 35, .5 mile north of I-90. ⊷ ⊼ 🏠 ♿

Midway: Where trail crosses County Road ZN. ⊷ 🏠

Lytles Landing: The end of County Road Z. ⊷ 🏠

When leaving the Onalaska access, you have to cross Highway 35 and follow marked city streets about .5 mile to the trail. From there the scenery becomes dramatic, starting with views of Lake Onalaska. This is followed by dry sand prairie (very colorful in late summer) just after Midway and before the Black River bridge. Lytles Landing is at one end of the 1226 foot bridge over the Black River, the longest Wisconsin trail bridge in this book. Now things get even wilder as you have water on both sides and views of the Mississippi River with the Minnesota bluffs in the background. During fall migration the skies here are busy.

TREMPEALEAU (to Trempealeau National Wildlife Refuge, 6 miles; to Marshland, 2.5 miles)

Trempealeau: Highway 35 and trail crossing east side of town. Well marked. ⊷ 🏠

Trempealeau National Wildlife Refuge: Exit Highway 35 at West Prairie Road. Go south to Refuge road. ⊷

Trempealeau, with its island mountain (the name means mountain "soaking in the water") is worth leaving the trail to see. The river, Perrot State Park, and Lock and Dam #6 will keep you busy for quite a while. Take any of the road crossings to get to the river. North of town is a signed spur trail into the state park. The pleasantness of the Great River Trail continues to Trempealeau National Wildlife Refuge, where to continue north you leave the right-of-way and use marked refuge roads, crossing the Trempealeau River in the process. The road doubles as an interpretive trail known as Wildlife Drive.

MARSHLAND

Marshland: One block east of the intersection of Highway 35 and County Road P. Look for a small sign. ⊷

Something Unique: Trempealeau National Wildlife Refuge and Wildlife Drive. Not many trails take you through a national wildlife refuge.

More Trail: The Great River State Park Trail continues south from the Onalaska access about 1.5 miles to and over the La Crosse River. From there a marked route takes you to the **La Crosse River State Park Trail.**

W7   La Crosse River State Park Trail

Wisconsin Department of Natural Resources
Primary: Crushed rock. 🚶 🚴 ♿ 🛷
Length: 21.5 miles.
Fees: Trail Admission Pass.
Recommendation: Medary to West Salem (7 miles). In the summer, enjoy the designated prairie three miles either side of Rockland.
FMI: La Crosse River State Trail
    Box 99
    Ontario, WI 54651
    608-337-4775

    La Crosse Convention and Visitors Bureau
    Riverside Park, Box 1895
    La Crosse, WI 54602
    608-782-2366

    Sparta Area Chamber of Commerce
    111 Milwaukee Street
    Sparta, WI 54656
    608-269-4123
    800-354-BIKE

General Trail Character: This trail connects the Elroy–Sparta State Park Trail at Sparta to the Great River State Park Trail at Onalaska with only minor and marked detours from the right-of-way at each end. The Wisconsin DNR has been a great purchaser of surplus railroad lands, and the abandonment of a Chicago and North Western Railroad made this trail possible. The trail parallels an active Canadian Pacific line, separated by 100 feet of vegetation and grade changes. An Amtrak train may whiz by at an 60 miles an hour. Highway I-90 is usually distant and does not disturb the experience much. The small towns along the way are worth exploring.

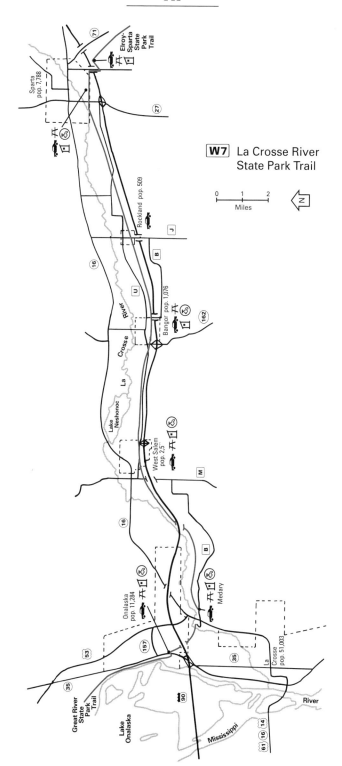

W7 La Crosse River State Park Trail

0   1   2
Miles

N

Sparta pop. 7,788

Elroy-Sparta State Park Trail

Rockland pop. 509

Bangor pop. 1,076

La Crosse River

Lake Neshonoc

West Salem pop. 2.5

Onalaska pop. 11,284

Medary

Great River State Trail

Lake Onalaska

Mississippi River

La Crosse pop. 51,003

La Crosse River

ONALASKA (to Medary, 1.5 miles; to West Salem, 7 miles)

Onalaska: Onalaska Center for Commerce and Tourism, right along State Highway 35, .5 mile north of I-90. Take the trail south. ⊷ ⼝ ⌁ ⬡

Medary: On County Road B, east of U. S. Highway 16. Well marked. ⊷ ⼝ ⌁ ⬡

From the Onalaska Access you have 1.5 miles of trail, then a .75 mile road detour to the Medary Access. From here you will notice the gentle climb to exit the La Crosse River valley to West Salem. Put up with it, as the next few miles are the nicest piece of trail. You'll find views of valley wetlands where the blanding turtle is known to inhabit. A golf course, woods, occasional picnic tables, and a trip under I-90 are along the way to West Salem. There are distance markers every .5 mile. At West Salem the well-developed Village Park has everything you need and is signed from the trail.

WEST SALEM (to Bangor, 5 miles; to Rockland, 3.5 miles; to Sparta, 6 miles)

West Salem: Village Park, center of town. ⊷ ⼝ ⌁ ⬡

Bangor: Village Park, southwest part of town. ⊷ ⼝ ⌁ ⬡

Rockland: Trail crosses County Road J. Street parking. ⊷

Toward Bangor is farm country and I-90. This village too has a trailside Village Park. Explore town and notice the dominating Hussa Brewery building. The prairie resources from Bangor to Rockland are biologically significant (over 350 species), are colorful (especially in late summer), and are managed as a natural area. Rockland has a strange rock outcrop in someone's backyard. It's south of the trail along the main north-south street. The environment of mixed woods, agriculture, and prairie continues to Sparta, "Bicycling Capital of America." You can complete your journey at the restored depot, now a trail center.

SPARTA (to the Elroy–Sparta State Park Trail, 1 mile)

Sparta: Trail Headquarters, one mile south of downtown on South Water Street. Well marked. ⊷ ⼝ ⌁ ⬡

You can continue east from the depot .5 mile on the right-of-way to a signed road route to the Elroy–Sparta State Trail southeast of town.

Something Unique: Amtrak and freight trains thundering. Stay away from the tracks.

More Trail: West of Medary is the **Great River State Park Trail.** To the southeast is the **Elroy–Sparta State Park Trail.**

W8   Mlilitary Ridge State Park Trail
Wisconsin Department of Natural Resources
Primary: Crushed rock. 🚶 🚲 🛶 ♿ ⚓
FYI: The 32-page *History and Guide: Military Ridge State Park Trail* is available for $1.00 from the DNR.
Length: 39.6 miles.
Fees: Trail Admission Pass.
Recommendation: Try Blue Mound to Barneveld (4 miles) or vice versa. Leave some time for the state park. For a longer trip do Blue Mounds to Riley or Verona.
FMI: Military Ridge State Park Trail
        4175 State Road 23
        Dodgeville, WI 53533
        608-935-5119 or 608-935-2315

        Dodgeville Chamber of Commerce
        P. O. Box 141
        Dodgeville, WI 53533
        608-935-5993

        Verona Area Chamber of Commerce
        P. O. Box 930003
        Verona, WI 53593
        608-845-5777

General Trail Character: The western two-thirds of this trail occupies the divide, called Military Ridge, between the Wisconsin River watershed to the north and the Pecatonica and Rock rivers to the south. The eastern third travels the Sugar River Valley. The highest point is at Blue Mounds, at 1300 feet, and the lowest is at Verona, at 930 feet. Settlement and railroads began in

W8 Military Ridge
State Park Trail

0   1   2
Miles

N

1827, when Henry Dodge mined lead, as had the Winnebago native Americans. Lead, used in everything from bullets to windows, was an incentive for better roads, so in 1835 Colonel Zachary Taylor (later President Taylor) supervised the construction of a military road on the ridge. By 1870 the emphasis had shifted to railroads, and the military ridge offered an excellent location. Construction began in 1880 by the Chicago and North Western Railway and was completed from Madison to Dodgeville in late 1881. Portions of the line were abandoned in 1979 and 1982. Now the trail, highways, towns, farms, and fields share the ridge and Sugar River Valley.

DODGEVILLE (to Ridgeway, 9.6 miles; to Barneveld, 5.2 miles; to Blue Mound, 3.9 miles)

Dodgeville: North side of town, near junction of State Highway 23 and County YZ. Go east on YZ .25 mile to well-marked access. ⛟

Ridgeway: Most anywhere along the loop off U. S. Highway 18 / 151. Street parking. ⛟

Barneveld: East side of town at City Park. ⛟

From Dodgeville east the trail's ridge location is obvious, and you can spot Blue Mounds State Park in the distance. At County Road Z you can head north on the paved shoulder to Governor Dodge State Park to enjoy its off-road paved trail system. The varied agricultural landscape continues as the trail wanders the ridge. Light woods and prairie grasses offer variety, and at times you are very close to busy Highway 18/151. The trail is the south boundary of the forested prairie mountain of Blue Mound State Park. A marked asphalt spur trail heads into the park.

BLUE MOUNDS (to Mt. Horeb, 5.1 miles; to Klevenville, 3.5 miles; to Riley, 2.5 miles; to Verona Access, 7.1 miles)

Blue Mounds: Mounds View Park, on the road to Blue Mound State Park. Follow signs toward the park. ⛟ ⚇ 🅿 ♿

Mt. Horeb: South side of downtown. Look for small signs. ⛟

Klevenville: No developed access. Street parking. ⛟

Riley: No developed access. Street parking. ⛟

The town of Blue Mounds is at the base of the towering, erosion-resistant Blue Mound. Downtown has funky old buildings, including Hooterville Inn. Spend some time on the trail, in the park, and around town. When you head east once again, the landscape opens up, and the highway returns. At Mt. Horeb, Troll Capital of the World, the trail passes through downtown, then leaves the ridge for the Sugar River valley. Here the experience is wilder, wetter yet, with that gentle rural and small-town touch. Klevenville and Riley have character but few services.

VERONA

Verona: East of town. From U.S. 18/151 exit south on County Road PB, go one block to marked access. 🛶

The Verona Access also doubles as an access to a portion of the Ice Age Trail for hiking.

Something Unique: It is possible to bike a loop using this trail, County Road Z, Governor Dodge State Park, and Highway 23.

More Trail: Governor Dodge State Park.

W9   Omaha Trail

Juneau County Land, Forestry and Parks Department
Primary: Asphalt emulsion. 🏃 🚲 🏕 ♿ 🛶
Length: 12.5 miles.
Fees: $1.00 per day, $5.00 per season.
Recommendation: Certainly do Elroy to the tunnel (5.5 miles). A shorter way there is to park at the County Road S crossing and go south 1.5 miles.
FMI: Juneau County Land, Forest and Parks
Department
250 Oak Street
Mauston, WI 53948
608-847-9389

Elroy Area Advancement Corp.
1410 Academy Street
Elroy, WI 53929
608-462-8545

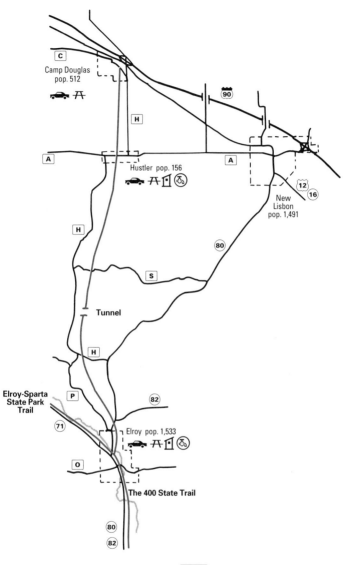

W9 Omaha Trail

0   1   2
Miles

N

General Trail Character: Peaceful is the best word for this trail and the countryside it traverses. Its claim to fame is its 875 foot tunnel. It is one of three trails radiating from the Commons park in Elroy. Connections from the Commons to the trail require using city streets. This line ended up as part of the Chicago and North Western Transportation Company. For years they operated the Chicago, St. Paul, Minneapolis, and Omaha Railroad, nicknamed the Omaha Road, which retained a separate corporate existence until 1972.

ELROY (to the tunnel, 5.5 miles)
Elroy: The Commons (downtown park) along State Highway 71. ➤ ⊼ 🅿 ♿

After you leave the busyness of the Commons you are probably alone as the trail is lightly used in summer. It is not long before you feel the tug of the 2% climb toward the tunnel 5.5 miles ahead. Mileage markers keep you informed of your progress. Like other trails running north-south this one has the disadvantage of being only lightly shaded even when flanked by thick woods. The trail also traverses wetlands, pastures, hills, and fields. The surface is moderately smooth and suitable for touring bicycles but not for in-line skates.

TUNNEL (to Hustler, 5 miles; to Camp Douglas, 2 miles)
Hustler: Downtown City Park, on County Road A. Street parking. ➤ ⊼ 🅿 ♿

This tunnel is a bit drier than the tunnels on the Elroy–Sparta State Park Trail. At the north end of the tunnel is a well-developed rest area. From here to County Road S you'll enjoy the descent. The landscape now opens up and flattens out as you head toward Hustler and beyond to Camp Douglas.

CAMP DOUGLAS
Camp Douglas: Downtown, on County Road 6. ➤ ⊼

More Trail: In Elroy the **Elroy–Sparta State Park Trail** is to the northwest, and to the south is the **400 State Trail.**

W10 Pecatonica State Park Trail
Tri-County Rails-to-Trails Commission
Primary: Limestone screenings. 🚶 🚲 ♿ 🛼
🐎

FYI: The trail is not completed between
Platteville and Belmont.
Length: 12 miles (not continuous).
Fees: Trail Admission Pass.
Recommendation: Belmont to Calamine (9.5
miles), especially the eastern half of this length.
FMI: Tri-County Rails-to-Trails Commission
  Ag Center
  627 Washington Street
  Darlington, WI 53530
  608-776-4830

  Platteville Chamber of Commerce
  275 Highway 151
  Platteville, WI 53818
  608-348-8888

General Trail Character: Time it right, and you can enjoy
blackberries as you amble along the Bonners Branch
of the Pecatonica River. From 1867 to 1869 the Mineral Point Railroad built this line as a branch of its
main route to the south. The extension to Platteville
was built in 1870 by the Dubuque, Platteville, and
Milwaukee Railroad. The whole route became part of
the Chicago, Milwaukee, and St. Paul Railroad in 1880.
Up to 12 combination trains a day traveled the valley.
The route was abandoned in 1974, and the Wisconsin
DNR purchased it the same year. Management is now
the responsibility of the Commission.

PLATTEVILLE (toward Belmont, 1 mile)
Platteville: East side of town at Mineral
Street and Valley Road intersection. Street
parking. 🚗

From Platteville the trail runs out of right-of-way after
a mile or so. Purchasing the whole route to Belmont
has not been possible yet. Although this stretch is
attractive, you don't have much choice but to turn
around or wander the interesting local roads.

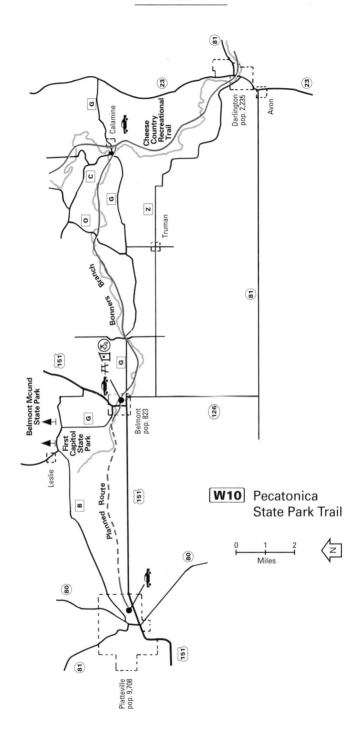

W10 Pecatonica State Park Trail

BELMONT *(to Calamine, 9.5 miles)*

Belmont: North side of downtown. Exit U.S. Highway 151 east on Market Street. Go one block to access in City Park. Note: To go west from the access you must cross the highway and follow Cushan Drive one block.

From Belmont the route is continuous and downhill 186 feet to Calamine. The valley is broad at first, lightly wooded and predominantly agricultural. The 24 bridges cross the creek and floodplain, and as you travel east, you get deeper and deeper into a wilder, more wooded, and isolated landscape. Travel prepared, as Calamine has no services.

CALAMINE

Calamine: West side of town along County Road G. Use Cheese Country Trail parking lot. Take Cheese Country 1 block south to Pecatonica, or use County Road G west across the bridge and another block.

Something Unique: Although not on the trail, 2 miles north of Belmont, is the Belmont Mound State Park, a erosion-resistant hill 160 feet above County Road G.

More Trail: This trail and the **Cheese Country Recreational Trail** join at a barely noticeable trail intersection 1 block south of the Calamine access.

W11 Red Cedar State Park Trail

Includes City of Menomonie Trail (W11-A)
Wisconsin Department of Natural Resources
Primary: Crushed rock.
Length: 14.5 miles.
Fees: Trail Admission Pass.
Recommendation: Start at Menomonie and enjoy the river and cliffs. Or try from the Dunnville Wildlife Area access south to the big bridge (2.5 miles). Don't miss Downsville.
FMI: Red Cedar State Park Trail
Route 6, Box 1
Menomonie, WI 54751
715-232-1242

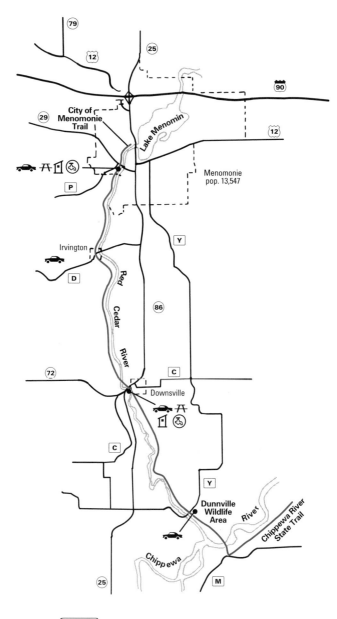

W11 Red Cedar State Park Trail
W11-A City of Menomonie Trail

Greater Menomonie Area Chamber
of Commerce
533 North Broadway
Menomonie, WI 54751
715-235-9087 or 1-800-283-1862

General Trail Character: The Red Cedar State Park Trail
is well maintained and comfortable for experiencing
the scenic Red Cedar River Valley from Menomonie
to the Chippewa River. This trail occupies the route
of the Red Cedar Junction Line, which was built by
Milwaukee Road in 1888 to connect the South Cedar
Falls Line with the Superior Railway Company Line.
Lumbering in Dunn County was big business for these
railroad routes hauled it to market. The line was sold
in 1882 to the Chicago, Milwaukee, St. Paul, and
Pacific Railroad Company and then was abandoned
in 1973. At Menomonie, the most used access, you
will find the Depot Visitor Center (offering pass sales,
interpretive displays, and restrooms), and an adjacent
city park with frontage on the Red Cedar River.
Another mile of trail to the north is being developed
and will be open soon.

**MENOMONIE *(to Irvington, 2.7 miles; to Downsville,
4.3 miles)***
Menomonie: West side of town along State
Highway 29. Well marked. 🚗 🏕 🎣 ♿
Irvington: Along County Road D. 🚗

When you head south from Menomonie, the trail
almost immediately travels below rock cliffs covered
with lush vegetation, and the river is close. At convenient intervals are picnic areas, often with views of
the river. Just north of Downsville, about milepost 7,
the trail crosses the Red Cedar on a steel bridge. Exit
the trail at Downsville to see the 1 block long
downtown.

**DOWNSVILLE *(to Dunnville Wildlife Area, 4.2 miles;
to Chippewa River, 2.5 miles)***
Downsville: Northwest side of town, where
County Road C crosses the trail. 🚗 🏕 🎣 ♿
Dunnville Wildlife Area: East of town along
County Road Y. 🚗

The attractiveness of the valley continues with occasional longer views dominated by prairie wildflowers,
forests, and marshes. Interpretive signs explain the

history of the Dunnville Quarries, which can be visited along mowed side paths. At about mile 11 is a wonderful rest area, and from here to County Road Y the river is close. The last and lower stretch of the Red Cedar State Trail takes you through the Dunnville Wildlife Area, with its extensive wetlands and flood-plain forests. This trail's conclusion is the impressive 800-foot bridge over the Chippewa River. In normal to low water you can reach the river at the bridge's north end.

Something Unique: A local legend claims that some-where near Irvington a company of French soldiers buried treasure along the river when they were threat-ened by Indians. The treasure has supposedly never been recovered!

More Trail: The **Chippewa River State Recreation Trail** is at the south end. To the north of the Menomonie access is the one mile long **City of Menomonie Trail.**

W12 Sugar River State Trail

Wisconsin Department of Natural Resources
Primary: Limestone screenings. 🚶 🚴 ⛷ ♿
🛶
Length: 23 miles.
Fees: Trail Admission Pass.
Recommendation: All visitors must explore New Glarus, a town with a rich Swiss heritage, and examine the Covered Bridge.
FMI: Sugar River State Trail
    P. O. Box 781
    New Glarus, WI 53574
    608-527-2334

    New Glarus Tourism Information
    Box 713U,
    New Glarus, WI
    608 527-2095

General Trail Character: The Sugar River State Trail has unique towns, a covered bridge, and outstanding rural scenery, with, a broad valley, remoteness, and frequent shade. The Sugar River Valley Railroad graded the Brodhead to Albany section in 1859 but then quit. The

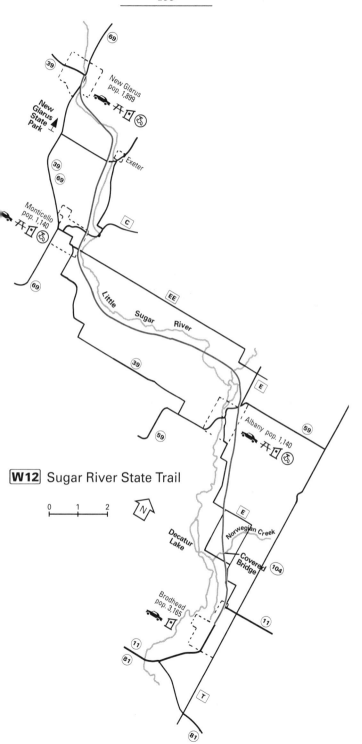

W12 Sugar River State Trail

Chicago, Milwaukee, and St. Paul Railroad Company finished the work to Albany in 1880 and to New Glarus in 1887. Several trains a day ran the line at first, but in the late 1940's service declined, and the Milwaukee Road abandoned it in 1972.

BRODHEAD (to Albany, 7 miles)
Brodhead: West side of downtown at 3rd Street. 🚗 🏠

The DNR access in Brodhead is not on the right-of-way, and you must take 3rd Street north (follow signs). Soon you are out of town, but a touch of surburbia lingers up to the covered bridge over Norwegian Creek. This bridge, just out of sight to the north from the south Golf Course Road crossing, is a 112-foot replica of a former 150 foot bridge originally located southwest of Brodhead. The replica was built using old barn wood with local labor and money. Follow the steps at the north end to get a better look.

ALBANY (to Monticello, 10 miles; to New Glarus, 6 miles)
Albany: East side of town where 4th Street crosses trail. 🚗 🏕 🏠
Monticello: East side of town on County Road EE. 🚗 🏕 🏠

You leave the occasionally parallel road at Albany and travel a flat valley to Monticello, through prairie, wetlands, woods, and wide curves. You cross both the Little Sugar and Sugar rivers on some of the trail's many trestles. There are mileage markers. A rolling agricultural landscape with enough shade extends north to the end at New Glarus Trail headquarters.

NEW GLARUS
New Glarus: Trail Headquarters Depot at intersection of State Highways 69 / 39.
🚗 🏕 🏠 ♿

Trail headquarters is in an 1887 restored depot, which offers amenities and information.

Something Unique: The covered bridge.

More Trail: From New Glarus south along Highways 69/39 there is an asphalt trail to the New Glarus Woods State Park (2 miles).

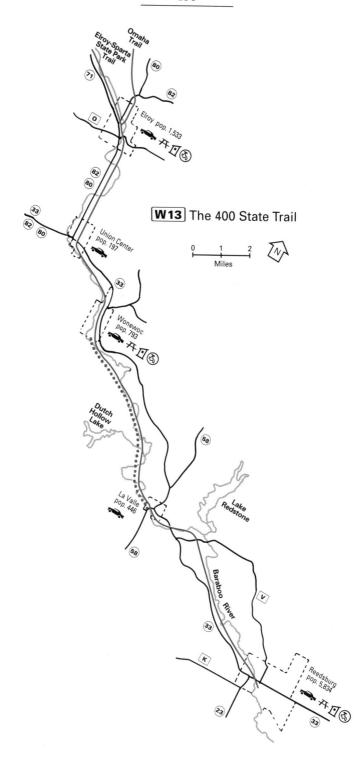

Omaha Trail

Elroy-Sparta State Park Trail

71

80

82

O

Elroy pop. 1,533

82
80

33
82 80

Union Center pop. 197

33

Wonewoc pop. 793

Dutch Hollow Lake

58

La Valle pop. 446

Lake Redstone

58

Baraboo River

33

V

W13 The 400 State Trail

0   1   2
Miles

N

K

Reedsburg pop. 5,834

23

33

W13 The 400 State Trail

Wisconsin Department of Natural Resources
Primary: Crushed rock. 🚶 🚴 ⛷ ♿ 🛷
Secondary: Natural. 🐾
FYI: Significant facility improvements are
under construction at the accesses in LaValle,
Wonewoc, and Union Center. Completion is
scheduled for spring, 1996.
Length: Primary: 22 miles.
　　　　Secondary: 7.5 miles.
Fees: Trail Admission Pass.
Recommendation: Union Center to Wonewoc
(4 miles) is a great introduction, and continu-
ing on to LaValle is also recommended.
FMI: The 400 State Trail
　　　　c/o Wildcat Mountain State Park
　　　　P. O. Box 99
　　　　Ontario, WI 54651
　　　　608-337-4775

　　　　Reedsburg Area Chamber of Commerce
　　　　210 East Main Street
　　　　Reedsburg, WI 53959
　　　　608-524-2850
　　　　800-844-3507

General Trail Character: The 400 State Trail is named
after the famous train route from Chicago to Minneapolis, completing 400 miles in 400 minutes. For years
the train roared through these communities carrying
passengers and freight. Eventually the line was abandoned by the Chicago and North Western Transportation Company and purchased by the Wisconsin DNR.

REEDSBURG (to LaValle, 8 miles; to Wonewoc, 7.5 miles)

Reedsburg: At the depot, south side of downtown. From State Highway 23/33 turn south
on Walnut Street South. Trail and depot in
about 2 blocks. 🚶 🏕 🏛 ♿
LaValle: West side of downtown where Commercial Street (State Highway 58) crosses. 🚶

Wisconsin trails often integrate themselves nicely with
the host communities. So it is at Reedsburg, where the
old brick depot in the middle of town is now the trail

access and chamber of commerce office. From here it is only a short ride through town to a rural landscape. In the 8 miles to LaValle you'll be pleasantly shaded and pleased by the qualities around you. Just north of LaValle is Hemlock Park, with a beautiful small lake and pine-covered sandstone bluffs. You will cross the Baraboo River so many times that keeping count is hopeless, but mileage markers record the distances. The LaValle to Wonewoc stretch of 7.5 miles has a parallel treadway for horses.

> **WONEWOC (to Union Center, 4 miles; to Elroy, 4 miles)**
> **Wonewoc:** Bakers Field Park, north side of town, marked from Highway 33. ➻ ⊼ 🏠 ♿
> **Union Center:** Anywhere along downtown. ➻

Wonewoc, the "Midpoint of the 400 Trail," has Baker Field Park on the north side as well as restrooms closer to the center of town. From the park north are numerous interpretive signs prepared by students in Wonewoc Center High School to explain the natural resources of the wild and wet landscape. Stop at R & A Liquidators in Union Center. You never know when they'll have something you need! The final four miles from Union Center to Elroy closely parallel Highway 80, with several more crossings of the Baraboo River.

> **ELROY**
> **Elroy:** The Commons (downtown park), along State Highway 71. ➻ ⊼ 🏠 ♿

Something Unique: Visible from the trail in Wonewoc is the Pets and More Store. This petting zoo and pet shop fills the proprietor's back yard and house.

More Trail: The **Elroy–Sparta State Park Trail** is to the northwest, and the **Omaha Trail** is to the north.

Wisconsin – Additional Rail-Trails

The rail trails listed here may be short, primarily of local interest, under develpoment, or only a small part of a longer trail. They are listed by management structure.

ASSOCIATION

W-A   Pine River Trail, Lone Rock to Richland Center
Length: 14.8 total, 14.8 Rail-Trail
Surface: Crushed rock
Primary uses: 🚶 🚲 ⛷ ♿
FMI: Backroad Bicycle
170 Richland Square
Richland Center, WI 53581
608-647-4636
Comments: This trail is the work of the Pine River Trail Association. Follows the Pine River and lower Wisconsin River. Completion planned for summer, 1996.

W-B   The Pine Line, Medford to Prentice
Length: 26.2 total, 26.2 Rail-Trail
Surface: Crushed rock (south 5.3 miles) remainder crushed gravel
Primary uses: 🚶 ⛷ 🐎
FMI: Medford to Prentice Rail Trail Association
111 East Division Street
P.O. Box 339
Medford, WI 54451
715-748-2030
Comments: Parallels Highway 13 through Taylor and Price counties. Connects with the Ice Age National Scenic Trail.

COUNTY

W-C   Oliver–Wrenshall Grade Trail, Douglas County
Length: 12.0 total, 6.5 Rail-Trail
Surface: Original ballast
Primary uses: 🚶 ⛷ 🏍
FMI: Douglas County Forestry Department
Box 211
Solon Springs, WI 54873
715-378-2219
Comments: This trail occupies former BN right-of-way and continues into Minnesota, connecting to the Alex Leveau Memorial Trail. No ATV use in Minnesota.

W-D   Soo Line Trail, Superior to state line
Length: 12.0 total, 10.0 Rail-Trail
Surface: Original ballast
Primary uses: 🚶 ⛷
FMI: see Oliver–Wrenshall Grade Trail
Comments: This trail occupies Soo line right-of-way which continues into Minnesota for a continuous trail of 114 miles.

W-E   **South Shore / Battleaxe / #63 and more,**
            Bayfield County
Length: varies
Surface: Original ballast
Primary uses: ⚓
FMI: Bayfield County Tourism Department
         Courthouse
         Box 832
         Washburn, WI 54891
         800-472-6338
Comments: The county has over 500 miles of trail with complex ownership patterns. Many use railroad corridors. As example, on Trail #63 the county owns 5 trestles, yet the grade between them is private and easements allow snowmobile use.

W-F   **Woodville Trail, Woodville to near Spring Valley**
Length: 7.0 total, 7.0 Rail-Trail
Surface: Original ballast
Primary uses: 🚶 🐴 ⚓
FMI: County Clerk Government Center
         1101 Carmichael Road
         Hudson, WI 54016
         715-386-4600
Comments: Former Chicago North Western right-of-way. Undeveloped.

MULTI-COUNTY

W-G   **Cattail Trail, Amery to Almena**
Length: 18.0 total, 18.0 Rail-Trail
Surface: Original ballast
Primary Uses: 🚶 🚲 ⚓ 🏇
FMI: Polk County Information Center
         Highway 35 & 8
         St. Croix Falls, WI 54024
         800-222-7655
Comments: Owned by the Wisconsin DOT, 12 miles are in Polk County and 6 in Barron County.

W-H   **Tri-County Corridor, Superior to Ashland**
Length: 61.8 total, 61.8 Rail-Trail
Surface: Original ballast
Primary uses: 🚶 ⚓ 🏇 🐴
FMI: Tourist Information Center
         305 Harbor View Parkway East
         Superior, WI 54880
         800-942-5313
Comments: Operated by the Tri-County Corridor Commission.

WISCONSIN DEPARTMENT OF NATURAL RESOURCES

W-I   **Old Abe State Recreation Trail, Chippewa Falls to Cornell**

Length: 20.0 total, 20.0 Rail-Trail
Surface: Original ballast
Primary uses: 🚶 🚴 🐎
FMI: Wisconsin DNR
        1300 West Clairmont Avenue
        P.O. Box 4001
        Eau Claire, WI 54702
        715-839-1607
Comments: Sometimes close to the Chippewa River.

W-J   **Tuscobia State Trail, Near Rice Lake to near Park Falls**

Length: 74.0 total, 73.0 Rail-Trail
Surface: Original ballast
Primary uses: 🚶 🐎 🏍
FMI: Tuscobia State Trail
        Wisconsin DNR
        Route 2, Box 2003
        Hayward, WI 54843
        715-634-6513
Comments: Some bridges are missing but detours are provided. A forested and wet landscape.

Endnote

Bits and pieces of abandoned and sometimes forgotten
railroad rights-of-way exist virtually everywhere you
look. Many, like those described and mentioned in
this book, end up being publicly owned and used for
some recreational purpose. It was not possible to
include all the known rail-trails in this edition of the
Rail-Trail Handbook. Undoubtedly there are others un-
known to the author. If you would like to see your
local rail-trail mentioned in the next edition, please
contact the author through the publisher.